The Structure of M&A Contracts

Kenneth A. Adams

The Structure of M&A Contracts

Kenneth A. Adams

■ CONTENTS

Click on any entry in the table of contents to go to that part of this book.

List of Figures

List of Tables

About the Author

Kenneth A. Adams is a consultant and speaker on contract drafting. He gives seminars in the U.S., Canada, and internationally, acts as a consultant and expert witness, and is a lecturer at the University of Pennsylvania Law School. His book *A Manual of Style for Contract Drafting* (ABA 2d ed. 2008) is widely used throughout the legal profession. As part of its "Legal Rebels" project, in 2009 the ABA Journal, the magazine of the American Bar Association, named Adams one of fifty leading innovators in the legal profession. And the ABA Journal included Adams's AdamsDrafting Blog in its 2009 and 2010 "Blawg 100"—its list of the hundred best law blogs.

Adams is also founder and president of Koncision Contract Automation, an online service that will make available to lawyers document-assembly templates for business contracts. He maintains at www.koncision.com his new blog, The Koncise Drafter.

After graduating from the University of Pennsylvania Law School in 1989, Adams practiced corporate law in New York and Geneva, Switzerland, with major U.S. law firms.

Foreword

First, do no harm. When drafting M&A contracts, attorneys too often violate this principle. Any given M&A contract is likely to be bloated, impenetrable, and haphazard in how it addresses some key issues. Instead of seeking to articulate the deal succinctly, drafters tack on clauses using *notwithstanding, provided however, for the avoidance of doubt,* and other warning signs of circumlocution. And drafters routinely seek to address every possible risk, even if doing so distracts attention from those that really matter. This is before negotiations, where the prevailing etiquette seems to require that each party pile on its own language to counter the other guy's.

When this drafting lands in court, it can get messy. The recent litigation between United Rentals and the private equity fund Cerberus provides a good example of that—confusion in the merger agreement resulted in an expensive fight over the remedies available to United Rentals on termination of the agreement.

The M&A world is currently subject to a perfect storm that makes it particularly susceptible to this kind of dispute. Compounding the tendency to dysfunction evident in business contracts generally is the fact that the pressures of M&A transactions favor expediency over meticulousness. On top of that, we have pressures due to the financial crisis—lawyers representing M&A clients can no longer assume that drafting glitches will be rendered irrelevant by the client's zeal to get the deal done.

The renewed focus on drafting is a welcome development. Historically, contract drafting has been treated as a craft that is learned on the job rather than as a discipline acquired through structured training, whether in law school or at a law firm. Corporate associates have learned how to draft by actually preparing and negotiating contracts. At the heart of the traditional system was the understanding that the only way to become truly proficient in M&A contracts is to immerse yourself in them. But due to lack of a truly rigorous framework for contract language and structure, the traditional system has too often become regurgitation of hand-me-down language.

The push for better contract drafting is in its infancy. Law firms are still debating how best to train lawyers. Law schools are, with varying levels of enthusiasm, taking steps to meet this need by offering courses in contract drafting and clinics in transaction skills. But there has been a dearth of relevant reference materials.

This is where Ken Adams comes in. Ken is a pioneer in this field. In particular, he's author of *A Manual of Style for Contract Drafting*. It's the leading reference work on the subject, and it's in use throughout the legal profession.

Ken has now turned his attention to M&A—hence this book. It's the basis for an eponymous webcast that he and I will be offering through West.

This book brings to bear on the structure of M&A contracts the same rigor, attention to detail, and disregard for sacred cows that informs *A Manual of Style for Contract Drafting*. It describes how to best address in M&A contracts issues related to structure that arise routinely in negotiation. And it does so with a clarity and comprehensiveness that cuts through the murk that surrounds much writing on these issues.

You might disagree with Ken's analysis of a given issue. But I suspect that when Ken encounters resistance, in large measure it's prompted by simple resistance to change. If you really do disagree with Ken, he'd be the first to invite you to do battle in the marketplace of ideas. As the intellectual underpinnings of M&A drafting become more robust, force of habit won't be enough to justify sticking with a given approach.

Ken acknowledges that resistance to a given change might make implementing that change more trouble than it's worth. But as drafting moves from craft to discipline, I expect that invoking that as a justification for the status quo will seem increasingly small beer.

So whether you're a junior lawyer striving for control in a tough field or a more senior practitioner revisiting M&A basics, I think you'll find this book uniquely valuable. It will help you draft contracts that more than satisfy the principle of "do no harm."

Steven M. Davidoff
N.Y. Times "Deal Professor"
Professor of Law, University of Connecticut School of Law

Preface

WHY THIS BOOK?

This book considers the function of the different categories of provisions in a mergers-and-acquisitions (or M&A) contract and the interplay among them. These are topics worthy of study: A slight change of phrasing in one part of a contract can have important implications for other parts of the contract. And issues relating to contract structure arise routinely in M&A negotiations.

This book is intended for anyone who wishes to understand the structure of M&A contracts. That obviously includes junior lawyers—they're the ones who do most of the drafting of M&A contracts. And they could certainly use some help. Many junior lawyers receive little formal training in the structure of M&A contracts, and what instruction they do receive likely features a generous helping of stale conventional wisdom. And the convulsions of the U.S. legal profession in recent years have made it less likely that a junior lawyer will receive meaningful mentoring. This book should help junior lawyers take control of the drafting process, instead of regurgitating precedent contracts of questionable quality and relevance. It should also help them understand what's going on during negotiations.

Senior lawyers who have the time and inclination to revisit how they handle the structure of M&A contracts should also find this book useful. And because other kinds of contracts—such as securities purchase agreements and loan agreements—can exhibit a structure comparable to that of M&A contracts, this book might be of interest to anyone involved in transactions featuring an interval between signing and closing.

The benefits of a clearer understanding of how to structure an M&A contract go beyond making life easier for the drafter. If those doing the drafting and reviewing have a better grasp of the subject, contracts would be clearer and would address the parties' concerns more effectively; negotiations would be more efficient and less contentious; and disputes would arise less frequently.

Others have written about the structure of M&A contracts, but five features serve to distinguish this book. First, its limited scope permits a more cohesive treatment than would be possible in a broader work. Second, rather than simply cataloguing the structures—good, bad, and indifferent—on display in M&A contracts, it identifies those that work best. Third, it specifies what contract language you should use in a given context and what contract language you should avoid; the recommended language complies with the guidelines contained in the author's *A Manual of Style for Contract Drafting*.[1] Fourth, it presents some of its analysis in a series of figures, so as to make it easier to understand. And fifth, it doesn't hesitate to depart from the conventional wisdom.

FEATURES OF THIS BOOK

This book refers to the buyer and seller in a hypothetical M&A contract. Who the seller is would depend on how the transaction is structured.[2] If it's a stock purchase, the seller is whoever owns the stock of the company being acquired—there might be more than one shareholder. If it's an asset purchase, the seller would be the company that owns the assets being acquired. In the case of a merger, it's inaccurate to refer to a seller, although the one or more shareholders of the company being acquired are analogous to sellers.

And this book focuses on provisions benefiting the buyer. Because to a greater or lesser extent the buyer assumes more risk than the seller, provisions benefitting the buyer necessarily predominate in any given M&A contract. But the categories of provisions can, to a greater or lesser extent, be structured to benefit either the buyer or the seller.

This book includes tables containing enumerated examples of contract language followed by variations. Each example is identified by a number in brackets; each variation is given the same designation but is distinguished by adding a lowercase letter. (For instance, [3b] denotes the second variation on example [3].) A given example or variation might be annotated to show whether it is recommended (✓) or contraindicated (✗). For consistency with the rest of the text, all examples are from a notional asset purchase agreement and so use the defined terms *the Buyer* and *the Seller*; you'd need to make conforming changes to some of them to use them for a transaction structured other than as an asset purchase.

At various points this book illustrates the frequency of a particular approach by indicating how often it appears in the M&A contracts included in the sample examined for the 2009 Private Target Deal Points Study,[3] a study conducted by the Mergers & Acquisitions Market Trends Subcommittee of the Committee on Mergers and Acquisitions of the Section of Business Law of the American Bar Association. Sometimes the 2009 Private Target Deal Points Study itself is cited; elsewhere, it is the author's own review of those contracts that is cited—the contracts are available through the subcommittee's page on the ABA's website.[4] It makes sense for this book to piggyback off of the Deal Points Study in that manner—those contracts would seem to constitute a representative cross-section, and they are conveniently accessible.

EFFECTING CHANGE

Some recommendations in this book are at odds with current practice. (Wherever that's the case, it's noted in the text.) That shouldn't dissuade you from following those recommendations. For one thing, a given approach may be enshrined in the dysfunction that is mainstream drafting,[5] but that doesn't mean that it's the most effective approach. In many cases, it clearly isn't.

Furthermore, one of the rewards of contract drafting is that the drafter has the opportunity to control meaning, as opposed to leaving it to the courts to make sense of murky contract language. If novel yet rigorous contract language addresses a flaw in the conventional approach and comes closer to expressing clearly the intent of the parties, you should consider using it. The alternative—sticking with current approaches because they've supposedly been "tested" by the courts—is unpromising. The caselaw is often patchy and even contradictory in its coverage of a given issue, varying from jurisdiction to jurisdiction and even within jurisdictions. And if any contract language came to be so tested, often it's because it failed to state clearly the intent of the parties. Why rely on language that resulted in litigation? Instead, express any given concept clearly, so you don't have to gamble on courts reading into your contract language the desired meaning.

But change is hampered by inertia. Deviating from standard language, no matter how defective, might spark debate, and debate creates delay and increases transaction costs. But inertia by itself isn't a valid reason to reject change—if it were, the precedent-driven nature of the transactional world would ensure that contract language remains fossilized. Instead, you have to weigh the time and money you might save through don't-rock-the-boat expediency against the increased efficiency and reduced risk offered by rigorous contract language; it shouldn't take much for the latter to outweigh the former. This book aims to help you see what's on each side of the equation.

A note to junior lawyers: before embracing the more novel recommendations made in this book, you should consider getting the approval of someone more senior.

COMMODITIZING

Drafting contracts takes up more lawyer time than it should. Because any transaction typically resembles previous transactions, drafting should be a commodity task, one powered by document-assembly software rather than by junior lawyers retooling word-processing documents. That would allow lawyers to focus on those tasks that add most value—devising strategy and assisting in negotiations.

But to commoditize, first you need broad consensus as to what contracts should look like. The author's goal in writing *A Manual of Style for Contract Drafting* was to propose a set of guidelines for contract usages. For purposes of commoditizing the process of drafting M&A contracts, equally important is a set of guidelines regarding structure. That's what this book provides.

ACKNOWLEDGMENTS

This book benefitted greatly from comments I received from Michael J. Kendall, Vincent R. Martorana, Brian J.M. Quinn, Steven H. Sholk, and Michael A. Woronoff. I offer them my thanks. And thank you to Wilson Chu for helping to make accessible to me the contracts examined for the 2009 Private Target Deal Points Study.

■ CHAPTER 1

The Categories of Provisions

1.1 Timing is a key factor in determining what categories of provisions an M&A contract should contain. If the transaction is consummated when the contract is signed—in other words, if the signing and closing are simultaneous—then the contract would usually contain deal provisions, representations, indemnification provisions, and boilerplate, as well as any postclosing obligations.

1.2 "Deal provisions" refers to those provisions that describe the core elements of the transaction.[6] "Boilerplate" refers to provisions that address interpretation of the contract and other matters typically relevant to contracts generally. They're also referred to as the "miscellaneous" provisions, and usually they're placed just before the concluding clause and the signatures. Deal provisions have limited bearing, and boilerplate has no bearing, on the interplay of different parts of a contract.

1.3 More relevant for purposes of structuring an M&A contract are representations and indemnification provisions. A representation is a statement of fact that one or more parties make so as to induce one or more other parties to enter into a contract.[7] And indemnification provisions grant a party the right to recover for inaccurate representations, noncompliance with obligations, and any other specified risks.[8] (Because enforcing indemnification obligations against public-company shareholders is problematic, indemnification is rare in public company transactions, except when a substantial shareholder agrees to indemnify the buyer.[9] This book assumes a context where indemnification would be appropriate.)

1.4 If the closing is scheduled to take place sometime after signing—in other words, if the closing is deferred—the contract would typically also contain obligations to be complied with before closing, conditions that have to be satisfied before the parties will be required to consummate the transaction, and termination provisions, which specify when a party may terminate the agreement. (Termination provisions can also serve the ancillary function of stating the terms of any breakup fee, but that function isn't a focus of this book.) Sometimes a contract contains these provisions even though the signing and closing are simultaneous. Presumably that's because originally it was thought that the closing might be deferred, and thereafter it was decided that stripping out the extra provisions would be more trouble than it was worth.

1.5 These additional components complicate matters, so this book focuses on contracts that provide for a deferred closing. More specifically, this book discusses representations, preclosing obligations, conditions, and indemnification provisions— James Freund's "four horsemen"[10]—as well as a fifth, termination provisions.

FIGURE 1: LINKS BETWEEN THE CATEGORIES OF PROVISIONS

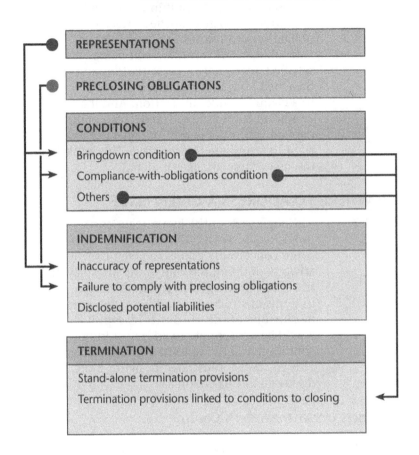

1.6   Figure 1 shows the links between these five categories of provisions: An inaccurate representation can result in the bringdown condition not being satisfied. Breach of an obligation can result in the compliance-with-obligations condition not being satisfied. Inaccurate representations and breached obligations can also give rise to a claim for indemnification. And if a condition cannot be satisfied, that could, depending on the condition, give rise to a right to terminate the contract. This book discusses these linkages in detail.

WHERE TO ADDRESS A GIVEN ISSUE

1.7   Although each of the five categories of provisions serves a different function, one could conceivably address a given issue in any one of them. But due to the interplay of the different categories, it's most efficient, in terms of structure, to address that issue in only one of the categories, except if it would be appropriate to address it in both a condition and the termination provisions. This concept is illustrated in figure 2 and discussed in this chapter.

Facts Under the Seller's Control

1.8   If a given issue relates to facts on the date of the agreement and those facts relate to matters that are under the seller's control (see the first main column in figure 2), it makes most sense to address that issue by having the seller make a representation as to those facts.

FIGURE 2: WHERE TO ADDRESS A GIVEN ISSUE

In a transaction with a deferred closing, a given issue could be addressed in a representation, a preclosing obligation, a condition, the indemnification provisions, or the termination provisions. Which approach makes most sense depends in part on the nature of the issue. Use of shaded text within thick borders indicates where it would be best to address a given issue.

	Fact Under the Seller's Control	Action Under the Seller's Control	Fact or Action by Person Not Under the Seller's Control	Economic Condition Not Under the Seller's Control
Seller Representations	The Seller is a corporation duly organized, validly existing, and in good standing under the laws of the state of Delaware.	The Seller has granted the Buyer and its representatives access to the Seller's premises between the date of this agreement and the Closing.	Acme has not terminated the Acme Contract.	The price of vanadium is at least $100 per gram.
Seller Preclosing Obligations	The Seller shall remain a corporation duly organized, validly existing, and in good standing under the laws of the state of Delaware.	The Seller shall grant the Buyer and its representatives access to the Seller's premises between the date of this agreement and the Closing.	The Seller shall cause Acme not to terminate the Acme Contract before the Closing.	The Seller shall cause the price of vanadium to be at least $100 per gram.
Conditions to the Buyer's Obligations	The Buyer's obligation to consummate the transaction contemplated by this agreement is subject to satisfaction of the following conditions:			
	that the Seller is a corporation duly organized, validly existing, and in good standing under the laws of the state of Delaware;	that the Seller has granted the Buyer and its representatives access to the Seller's premises between the date of this agreement and the Closing;	that Acme has not terminated the Acme Contract;	that the price of vanadium is at least $100 per gram;
Indemnification	The Seller shall indemnify the Buyer against any Indemnifiable Losses arising from the following:			
	the Seller's not being a corporation duly organized, validly existing, and in good standing under the laws of the state of Delaware;	the Seller's not granting the Buyer and its representatives access to the Seller's premises between the date of this agreement and the Closing;	Acme's terminating the Acme Contract before the Closing;	the price of vanadium being less than $100 per gram;
Termination	This agreement may be terminated as follows:			
	by the Buyer if the Seller ceases to be a corporation duly organized, validly existing, and in good standing under the laws of the state of Delaware;	by the Buyer if the Seller fails to grant the Buyer and its representatives access to the Seller's premises between the date of this agreement and the Closing;	by the Buyer if Acme terminates the Acme Contract before the Closing;	by the Buyer if the price of vanadium is less than $100 per gram;

(For why it would be appropriate to address the issue in the third main column in both a condition and the termination provisions but would be most efficient to address the issue in the fourth main column only in a condition, see 1.16, 6.6, and figure 7.)

1.9   If that representation were made both on the date of the agreement and at closing (see 2.24–28), the buyer wouldn't also need to impose a preclosing obligation on the seller to undertake to ensure that those facts remain accurate between the date of the agreement and closing. But the subject matter of a given representation may be such that the buyer would be keen to have consistency between the date of the agreement and closing. (One such representation might be a representation that the seller has all permits required by law—it could be problematic if one or more permits were to lapse temporarily between the date of the agreement and closing.) Typically such issues are addressed both in a representation and in an obligation related to operation of the target business between signing and closing. (See 3.2.)

1.10   From the buyer's perspective, if a given issue relates to facts at the time the contract is signed and those facts relate to matters that are under the seller's control, addressing that issue only in a condition has the disadvantage of not entitling the buyer to damages if the condition isn't satisfied. And if this issue were addressed in a representation, it would be superfluous also to address it specifically in a condition, as an optimally drafted bringdown condition would serve to make accuracy of that representation a condition to closing. (See 4.17.)

1.11   If the issue were addressed in a representation, it would be unnecessary also to address it in a termination provision, as an optimally drafted set of termination provisions would specify that inability to satisfy the bringdown condition constitutes grounds for termination. (See 6.7.)

1.12   And the buyer should be indemnified against losses arising from inaccurate representations. (See 5.2.) If that's the case, nothing would be gained by also providing that the seller must indemnify the buyer for inaccuracies in one or more specific representations.

Action Under the Seller's Control

1.13   If the issue in question relates to an action to be taken by the seller between the date of the agreement and closing (see the second main column in figure 2), one could address it in a representation with the period between signing and closing as a reference period. (See 2.57.) But it's clumsy to have a seller make representations as to future facts—if you make a representation regarding the future, you're not so much stating facts as gazing into a crystal ball. In this context, it would be more straightforward to impose on the seller a preclosing obligation to accomplish that action.

1.14   As with facts under the seller's control, it would be to the buyer's disadvantage to address solely by means of a condition an action under the seller's control, as the buyer wouldn't be entitled to bring a claim for indemnification if the condition weren't satisfied. And it would serve no purpose to address in both an obligation and a condition an action under the seller's control, as the compliance-with-obligations condition would serve to make performance of that action a condition to closing. (See 4.41.) It follows that it would also serve no purpose to address such an action specifically in the termination provisions—a contract should provide that inability to satisfy the compliance-with-obligations condition constitutes grounds for termination. (See 6.7.) And the buyer should be indemnified if the seller fails to comply with its obligations (see 5.2), so nothing would be gained by also providing that the seller must indemnify the buyer if it fails to comply with a specific obligation.

Facts or Action Not Under the Seller's Control

1.15   The issue in question might not be under the seller's control, either because it's entirely or partly under the control of someone else or because it relates to general economic conditions. (See the third and fourth main columns of figure 2.) In either case, it would be illogical for the seller to make a representation regarding that issue: even if the seller could determine that the representation was accurate at signing, it would have no way of controlling changes between the date of the agreement and closing. Similarly, it would be futile to impose on the seller a preclosing obligation to ensure that someone over whom the seller has no control takes a specified action, or that facts over which the seller has no control are accurate at closing.

1.16   Instead, it would be more appropriate to address the issue in a condition to closing that requires that the event have occurred before the closing, or that the facts be accurate at closing. And the issue shouldn't also be addressed in the indemnification provisions—if a condition to the buyer's obligation to close isn't satisfied, the buyer wouldn't be entitled to bring a claim for indemnification. Whether you'd also address the issue in a termination provision, and how, would depend on the nature of the condition. (See 6.4–11.) That's why in figure 2 only one of the two issues highlighted as most appropriately addressed in a condition is also addressed in a termination provision.

1.17 One could argue that it would nevertheless be preferable to address in a representation or preclosing obligation matters over which a party has no control, because then the buyer could sue for damages if the representation were inaccurate or the obligation had been breached. But that assumes that rather than recharacterizing it as a condition, a court would take such a representation or preclosing obligation at face value—an uncertain proposition. It would be clearer to address this sort of risk allocation through the indemnification provisions or a negotiated breakup fee.

■ CHAPTER 2

Representations

FUNCTION

2.1 If the seller makes in a contract a representation that later proves to have been inaccurate, the buyer could—depending on the nature of the representation and procedural requirements under applicable law—have a cause of action for misrepresentation or breach of warranty, or both. But in M&A contracts it's standard to provide that indemnification is the exclusive remedy.[11]

THE REPRESENTATIONS LEAD-IN

2.2 Any set of representations is preceded by an introductory phrase, or "lead-in." This book recommends that you use example [1] as your representations lead-in. Drafters use many suboptimal variations.

TABLE 1: THE REPRESENTATIONS LEAD-IN

[1]	✓	The Seller represents to the Buyer as follows and will be deemed to have so represented again at Closing:
[1a]	✗	The Seller represents to the Buyer as follows:

[1b]   ✗   The Seller represents to the Buyer as follows, on the date of this agreement and as of the Closing:

[1c]   ✗   The Seller represents and warrants to the Buyer ... :

[1d]   ✗   The Seller hereby represents to the Buyer as follows ... :

[1e]   ✗   The Seller makes to the Buyer the following representations ... :

[1f]   ✗   As a material inducement to the Buyer to enter into this agreement, with the understanding that the Buyer will be relying thereon in consummating the transactions contemplated by this agreement, the Seller represents to the Buyer as follows ... :

[1g]   ✗   The Seller represents to the Buyer as follows... except to the extent those representations expressly relate to a specific date, in which case the Seller is making those representations as of that date:

[1h]   ✗   The Company represents to the Buyer ... that the following statements are and will be true and correct [in all material respects]:

[1i]   ✗   Except as stated in the corresponding sections of the Seller Disclosure Schedules, the Seller represents to the Buyer ... :

[1j]   ✗   The Sellers jointly and severally represent to the Buyer ... :

Making Representations on the Date of the Agreement

2.3   Because the buyer is relying on the seller's representations regarding what's being acquired, the buyer would want the seller to stand behind the accuracy of its representations on entry into the contract. If the deal doesn't close and any of the seller's representations are found to have been inaccurate, the buyer would want to be able to bring a claim for indemnification.

2.4   For the seller to make representations on entry into the contract, it's not necessary to state expressly when the representations are being made. It's sufficient to say, as in [1], *The seller represents ... as follows.* That assertion is necessarily being made on entry into the contract—in other words, on the date of the agreement.

Making Representations Only on the Date of the Agreement

2.5   The author has determined that of the 90 contracts in the 2009 Private Target Deal Points Study sample (see "Preface—Features of this Book") that exhibit a structure consistent with a deferred closing, in 55 the representations lead-in is silent as to when the representations are being made and in five it is stated, redundantly (see 2.4), that the representations are being made only on the date of the agreement. So in 60 of the contracts, or 66.7%, the representations are being made only on the date of the agreement and not also at closing. That's consistent with the author's informal survey of a sample of M&A contracts filed on the Securities and Exchange Commission's EDGAR system, a majority of which had the seller making representations on the date of the agreement but not also at closing.

2.6 In any contract reflecting that approach, the buyer might, by operation of the bringdown condition, be able to walk if one or more representations would have been inaccurate if they had been made again at closing. (See 4.17.) But absent any workaround, that approach would result in the buyer's being unable to bring a claim for indemnification based on the fact that one or more representations would have been inaccurate if made again at closing.

2.7 Consistent with this, *Negotiated Acquisitions of Companies, Subsidiaries and Divisions* states that "If a representation is not true at closing (but was true at signing), the representing party cannot be sued for it; the other party can merely refuse to close." But it goes on to say, "This can be resolved in the buyer's favor if the indemnification provisions are properly drafted or if the representations (either each one or a general representation) provide that the situation as represented is true at signing and 'at Closing, will be true.'"[12]

2.8 If in accordance with that suggestion you include the closing as a reference point in a representation (see 2.56), then on entry into the contract the seller would be asserting the accuracy of facts at closing. Although that would give the buyer a basis for at least arguing that it's entitled to recover damages due to inaccuracy at closing,[13] representing

14

on entry into the contract regarding facts at closing is somewhat awkward compared with representing at closing as to accuracy of those facts. (See 1.13.) Furthermore, it would be particularly inefficient to include the closing as a reference point in each representation.

2.9   As for stating in a separate representation that the representations will be accurate at closing, that approach exhibits flawed logic. A representation made on the date of the agreement is accurate or inaccurate with respect to that date only. It doesn't make sense to refer to it as remaining accurate, or becoming inaccurate due to developments occurring after the date of the agreement—it will always be accurate, but with respect to that date only. It follows that representations made on the date of the agreement have no bearing on the state of affairs at closing, which would be covered only by representations made at closing. So instead of saying that the seller's representations made on the date of the agreement will be accurate at closing, you should have the seller make the representations again at closing.

2.10   Another way to try to work around the implications of omitting from the representations lead-in any reference to the closing is to rely on the officer's certificate delivered by the seller.

2.11   Typically an M&A contract will provide for the seller to deliver at closing an officer's certificate—also referred to in contracts as a "compliance certificate" or "closing certificate"—regarding satisfaction of the conditions to the buyer's obligation to consummate the transaction. Usually the officer's certificate tracks the wording of the conditions.

2.12   Two provisions pertinent to the officer's certificate are (1) the provision—in the form of a preclosing obligation or, preferably, a condition (see 4.13)—calling for the seller to deliver the officer's certificate and (2) the indemnification provisions.

2.13   The basic form of provision calling for delivery of the officer's certificate requires the seller to deliver a certificate stating that the seller has satisfied the bringdown condition, the compliance-with-obligations condition, and any other relevant condition. That language is appropriate, as it reflects the core function of the officer's certificate as it relates to the bringdown condition.[14] The author has determined that of the 85 contracts in the 2009 Private Target Deal Points Study sample (see "Preface—Features of this Book") that provide for delivery of an officer's certificate without simply referring to a form attached as an exhibit, 48, or 56.6%, use this approach.

2.14   As regards indemnification provisions, it's standard for the buyer to be entitled to indemnification for losses arising from inaccurate seller representations. (See 5.2.) It follows that in order for the buyer to be entitled to indemnification for an incorrect statement in the seller officer's certificate, the buyer would have to be able to characterize that statement as a representation.

2.15   But if the contract states that the purpose of the officer's certificate is to confirm that conditions have been satisfied, it's hard to see, as a matter of logic, how one could characterize as a representation a statement in an officer's certificate regarding accuracy of the seller's representations. For one thing, that would allow you to use an officer's certificate to turn any condition into a representation.

2.16   So despite assertions to the contrary,[15] it's far from clear that having the seller deliver an officer's certificate at closing is equivalent to having the seller restate its representations at closing, thereby allowing the buyer to bring a claim for indemnification under the contract, as opposed allowing the buyer to seek some other remedy, for example a claim for fraud.[16]

2.17   But tweaking the contract language can muddy the waters. For one thing, variant forms of the provision calling for the seller to deliver an officer's certificate could be used to make it easier to argue that a statement in an officer's certificate constitutes a representation for purposes of indemnification.

2.18   Instead of saying that the officer's certificate serves to state that conditions have been satisfied, many such provisions refer to delivery of a certificate "to the effect set forth" in the bringdown condition, or words to similar effect. For example, the second edition of the *Model Stock Purchase Agreement* published by the American Bar Association's Section of Business Law refers to receipt of a certificate confirming accuracy of each seller's representations "in accordance with" the bringdown condition.[17] (The author has determined that 27, or 31.8%, of the 85 relevant contracts in the 2009 Private Target Deal Points Study sample use this approach. See 2.13.) Or such provisions track the language of the bringdown condition. (The author has determined that 10, or 11.8%, of the 85 relevant contracts in the 2009 Private Target Deal Points Study sample use this approach.) By not stating that the function of the officer's certificate is to confirm that conditions have been satisfied, you leave open the possibility that it has some additional function.

2.19   Or you could be explicit on that point. For example, one of the contracts in the 2009 Private Target Deal Points Study sample states, after the condition regarding delivery of a seller officer's certificate, that the statements contained in the officer's certificate "will be a representation and warranty of the Holding Company which will survive the Closing as provided in Article 10"—in other words, it could form the basis for a claim for indemnification.

2.20   Furthermore, indemnification provisions can be worded so as to make it easier to argue that a statement in an officer's certificate constitutes a representation for purposes of indemnification. That's presumably what *Negotiated Acquisitions of Companies, Subsidiaries and Divisions* has in mind in saying that the buyer can bring a claim for inaccuracy at closing "if the indemnification provisions are properly drafted" (see 2.7).[18]

2.21   Many indemnification provisions refer to accuracy of not only representations stated in the contract proper, but also, among other things, any certificate. And you could be even more specific and have the indemnification provisions cover representations in an officer's certificate. For example, included in the representations covered by the indemnification provisions in the *Model Stock Purchase Agreement* is any representation contained in the "bring down certificate" delivered by the sellers.[19]

2.22   So if the seller makes its representations only on the date of the agreement and it turns out that one or more seller representations were inaccurate at closing, there's room for the buyer to argue that it's entitled to bring a claim for indemnification based on the seller officer's certificate, with the strength of its argument depending on the wording used in the contract. And caselaw suggests that courts might be willing to hold that a certificate to the effect that a condition has been satisfied itself constitutes a representation for purposes of indemnification.[20]

2.23   But regardless of how the contract is worded, the core function of the seller officer's certificate is to confirm that conditions have been satisfied. That makes it unavoidably awkward to use the officer's certificate as a basis for bringing a claim for indemnification if one or more representations would have been inaccurate if they had been made again at closing. And not only awkward, but also unnecessary, given that a much simpler and clearer alternative exists.

Making Representations Also at Closing

2.24   A more straightforward way to ensure that the buyer is entitled to indemnification with respect to inaccuracies in seller representations not only on the date of the agreement but also at closing is to make it explicit that the seller stands behind accuracy of its representations not only when the agreement is entered into but also at closing. That could conceivably be accomplished three different ways.

2.25   First, the parties could make it a condition to closing that the seller make again at closing the representations that it had made on the date of the agreement. But that would require a new closing document or would require adjusting the officer's certificate, given that it doesn't currently serve that function and is signed by an officer of the seller rather than by the seller itself. Furthermore, having the seller actually restate its representations goes against a principal assumption underlying deferred closings, which is that at closing the buyer will have the benefit of the bargain it made with the seller at signing. So the seller should instead commit *at signing* to standing behind its representations at closing.

2.26   Second, as in [1b] the seller could state at signing that it's making its representations not only on the date of the agreement but also *as of the Closing*—in other words, as if it were making them at closing. The author has determined that of the 90 contracts in the 2009 Private Target Deal Points Study sample (see "Preface—Features of this

Book") that exhibit a structure consistent with a deferred closing, 25, or 27.8%, use this approach and another four do so using to the same effect the defined term *Effective Time* or *Effective Date*, for a total of 29 contracts, or 32.2%. Although it has economy in its favor, this approach requires that the parties in effect pretend that the day the seller is making its representations is not only the date of the agreement but also when the closing occurs. That doesn't make sense.

2.27 Third, the parties could use a different legal fiction and say, as in [1], that the seller will be deemed to have made the representations at closing.[21] This book recommends that approach—it's unorthodox, but it reflects the logic underlying a deferred closing better than the second alternative.

2.28 Example [1] doesn't use the phrase *the Closing Date*—because nothing stands in the way of referring to the closing itself, no purpose would be served by suggesting that the seller is making its representation at some unspecified time during the day on which the closing occurs.

2.29 The word *closing* is problematic, too, in that it's ambiguous—depending on the context, it's used to refer to either the closing process or the moment the transaction is consummated. It would be preferable if in M&A contracts *closing* were defined to mean only the moment the transaction is consummated, because that meaning fits the way *Closing* is used in the representations lead-in and in the bringdown condition (see 4.17). So in this book, *closing* is used to convey that meaning.

2.30   But for purposes of a merger, *Closing* would have to be defined to mean the moment when one or both certificates of merger, as applicable, are accepted for filing, unless the certificate of merger gives a later date for effectiveness of the merger. It's conventional in merger agreements to use the defined term *Effective Time* to convey that meaning, but it's problematic to use in a contract two defined terms with essentially the same meaning.[22]

2.31   Because the moment a transaction is consummated represents not a period of time but the boundary between the preclosing period and the postclosing period, strictly speaking you'd be making representations not *at* closing but *immediately before* closing. But it would be unduly formalistic to insist on reflecting that in the representations lead-in.

"Represents and Warrants"

2.32   Most drafters use the couplet *represents and warrants* in the representations lead-in, as in [1c], and elsewhere in a contract refer to *representations and warranties*. Others use *representations and warranties* in the representations lead-in too, although that's more cumbersome. (See 2.45.) The result is that the overwhelming majority of drafters use one or other couplet in the representations lead-in. The author has determined that of the 106 contracts in the 2009 Private Target Deal Points Study sample (see "Preface—Features of this Book"), all use in the representations lead-in either *represents and warrants* or *representations and warranties*, except for one, which uses *represents*.

2.33   One explanation offered for this usage is that a party may bring a tort claim for misrepresentation due to an inaccurate statement of fact in a contract only if that statement constitutes a representation, and to constitute a representation a statement of fact must in the contract be introduced by *represents* or be referred to as a representation. And a party may bring a contract claim for breach of warranty only if that statement constitutes a warranty, and to constitute a warranty a statement must in the contract be introduced by *warrants* or be referred to as a warranty.[23] So a party relying on statements of fact in a contract would, according to this explanation, want those statements to be introduced by both *represents* and *warrants*, so that it might avail itself of either or both remedies.

2.34   But that notion is unhelpful, as it relies on a "magic words" approach to contract language, with words being given a secondary meaning not evident to most readers.[24] In standard English, the verbs *represent* and *warrant* simply serve to indicate which party is stating a given set of facts, but proponents of the "magic words" approach would have each verb do double duty by having them also determine the remedies available if a statement of fact turns out to have been inaccurate.

2.35   The "magic words" approach results in there being attributed to contract language meaning that likely was unintended. Use of the phrase *represents and warrants* with respect to statements of fact is just another example of the lawyer penchant for stringing words together when one word would do.[25] It's futile to try to attribute to words a meaning not contemplated by those who use them. One indication that drafters don't have remedies in mind when they use the couplet *represents and warrants* is that it's routinely used even in contracts that provide for indemnification as the exclusive remedy.

2.36   The remedies implications of *representation* and *warranty* come into play only in litigation. In that context, *representation* makes most sense as shorthand for "a statement of fact capable of supporting an action for misrepresentation" and *warranty* makes most sense as shorthand for "a statement of fact capable of supporting an action for breach of warranty." When used to convey those meanings, both terms are labels applied after the fact. That's very different from suggesting that when those words are used in contracts they serve to dictate remedies.

2.37   Given that the "magic words" explanation for *represents and warrants* is inconsistent with how English works, it should come as no surprise that no U.S. caselaw supports it. In fact, courts take the opposite approach, as does the Uniform Commercial Code.[26] (Some English caselaw endorses it, but that's because the English legal profession is, to its detriment, particularly susceptible to the "magic words" approach to contract language.)[27]

2.38 Even if the "magic words" approach were more widely accepted, it would always be inferior to saying clearly in a contract what you mean to say. If you wish to specify the remedies for inaccurate statements of fact, do so without relying on *represents and warrants* to convey a secondary meaning.

2.39 Because it's consistent with standard English to consider that the verb preceding statements of fact serves only to indicate who is making those statements, it follows that it would be preferable to use one verb, not two. Your best bet is *represents*—it can be used with all assertions of fact, whereas the verb *warrant* is used on its own primarily in sales contracts and is also used to express obligations.[28] It's unlikely that practitioners would embrace some novel alternative, such as *asserts*. And for a noun, use *representation*.

2.40 You sometimes see *represents, warrants, covenants, and agrees*. Just as you should omit *warrants*, you should also omit the archaic *covenants*—what follows are statements of fact, not obligations.[29] And omit also *agrees*— the lead-in to the contract states that the parties are agreeing to everything in the body of the contract, so it's redundant to state in the body of the contract that a party agrees to a given provision.[30] Furthermore, it's odd to say that a party agrees to its own representations.

2.41 Even if a usage is superior to entrenched language, drafters will be inclined to use it only if the advantages it offers overcome inertia. (See "Preface—Effecting Change.") In one respect, the benefits of dispensing with *represents and warrants* are limited:

because no caselaw supports the "magic words" approach, U.S. courts can be counted on not to attribute any significance to use of *represents and warrants* as opposed to *represents* or *warrants* on its own. But continued use of *represents and warrants* nevertheless has the potential for mischief, in that anyone who endorses the "magic words" approach has a confused view of how remedies work and, more broadly, how contract language operates.

2.42 Dropping *represents and warrants* in favor of *represents* could conceivably prompt debate resulting in delay and increased transaction costs. But because as a matter of law and semantics the "magic words" approach lacks any support, there's nothing to debate. That's unlikely to stop people from questioning the change, at least initially, but it should help cut short any discussion. In that regard, providing them with a copy of this analysis might save you some time.

2.43 So on balance, the benefits of sticking with *represents and warrants* are outweighed by the benefits of eliminating this pointless and confusing usage.

"Hereby Represents"

2.44 It's commonplace for a contract to state that a party *hereby represents*, as in [1d], rather than simply *represents*. The word *hereby* is used to signal that the act described is being accomplished by means of the provision itself, as in *Acme hereby grants the license to Widgetco*. But in standard English *hereby* is used less often with verbs of speaking, such as *represents,* as compared to verbs expressing action, so this book recommends that you not say *hereby represents.*[31]

Using a Verb Instead of a Verb and Abstract Noun

2.45   In the representations lead-in you could use the formula *makes ... the following representations,* as in [1e], instead of *represents ... as follows.* The author has determined that of the 106 contracts in the 2009 Private Target Deal Points Study sample (see "Preface—Features of this Book"), six, or 5.7%, use that approach (albeit with *representations and warranties* rather than *representations;* see 2.32). But using a verb is more concise than using a verb and an abstract noun.[32]

Reliance

2.46   Nothing is accomplished by stating in the representations lead-in, as in [1f], that the buyer is relying on the seller's representations. Such language states the obvious and should be omitted.

Reference-Point Exception

2.47   When representations are being made on the date of the agreement and at closing, sometimes the lead-in makes an exception for representations that contain a reference point; see [1g]. But such language misconstrues the role of a reference point. Including a reference point in a representation doesn't alter the fact that the representations are being made on the date of the agreement and at closing. (See 2.58.) Regarding analogous and equally problematic language that drafters sometimes include in the bringdown condition, see 4.40.

Accuracy

2.48 In some contracts the representations lead-in has the party in question representing, as in [1h], that the statements being made are accurate. Such language is redundant—if in a contract a party makes statements of fact, that party is implicitly also asserting that those facts are accurate.

2.49 Such assertions of accuracy can incorporate a materiality qualification; see [1h]. (Regarding materiality qualifications in representations, see 2.76–91.) But many buyers would presumably reject such an across-the-board materiality qualification of the seller's representations—the author has determined that of the 106 contracts in the 2009 Private Target Deal Points Study sample (see "Preface—Features of this Book"), only one uses that approach.

Exceptions for Matters Stated in Disclosure Schedules

2.50 It's standard for a party's representations to be subject to exceptions stated in a set of disclosure schedules prepared by that party. (See 2.72.) The least clear way of alerting the reader that representations are subject to exceptions is to say so only in the representations lead-in, as in [1i]—that forces the reader to continually consult the disclosure schedule to determine which representations are subject to exceptions.

Instead, if a given representation is subject to one or more exceptions stated in a disclosure schedule, say so in the representation by referring to the relevant section of the disclosure schedule. If you do so, nothing would be gained by also saying in the representations lead-in that the representations that follow are subject to exceptions.

2.51 Drafters routinely include in the representations lead-in language—as much as several lines' worth—relating to the structure and interpretation of the disclosure schedules. Such language clogs the lead-in; the boilerplate would be a much better place for it. (You could instead put it immediately before the disclosure schedules,[33] but it seems inefficient to place this one group of substantive provisions apart from the body of the contract.)

When More Than One Party Makes a Set of Representations

2.52 When a set of representations is being made by more than one party, you can address that in the representations lead-in in one of two ways. First, you can have the parties make the representations collectively, as in *The Sellers represent to the Buyer and Able, Baker, and Charlie represent to the Buyer.* Second, if the representing parties are referred to by means of a collective defined term such as *the Shareholders*, you can say *Each Shareholder represents to the Buyer.*

2.53 The implications of having each member of a given group make a set of representations rather than the members of that group collectively depends on the nature of those representations. The representations might refer only to facts pertaining to the group member making the representations. For example, a shareholder might make representations regarding its ownership of shares being acquired, with each representation referring to *that Shareholder*. In the case of any such representations, the group member is making only representations as to itself and wouldn't be liable for inaccurate representations made by any other group member as to that other group member. If that's the nature of the representations, it's appropriate to flag that by adding to the lead-in the words *as to itself*, as in, for example, *Each Shareholder represents to the Buyer as to itself.*

2.54 Alternatively, each group member rather than the group collectively can make a set of representations even if the representations relate to more than just the representing group member. But in that case, saying, for example, *Each Seller represents to the Buyer* is functionally identical to saying *The Sellers represent to the Buyer.* It would be clearer to have the group members make the representations collectively, having the lead-in instead refer to an individual group member just when each group member is making representations only as to itself.

2.55 When more than one party is making a set of representations, it's common practice for drafters to use in the representations lead-in the couplet *jointly and severally*, as in [1j].[34] But *joint and several* applies to liability—it means that a given liability can be apportioned equally among the members of a group or can, to a greater extent or entirely, be laid at the door of one or more members of the group, at the discretion of whoever is apportioning the liability.[35] In an acquisition agreement, the place to allocate liability among a group of parties is in the indemnification provisions. Doing so would render it unnecessary—in fact illogical—to have those parties also make their representations jointly and severally.[36] And it follows that the representations lead-in also isn't the place to say that the members of a given group are severally but not jointly liable.

THE REFERENCE POINT

2.56   In addition to the question of when a party is making its representations (see 2.3–31), there is also the question of whether to provide what this book terms a "reference point" for a given representation—in other words, whether to have the representation speak as to accuracy of facts only at a point in time stated in the representation. A reference point will usually be expressed as a given day, although if greater precision is required one could also specify a time of day.[37]

2.57   A representation might speak as to accuracy of facts not at a reference point but during a "reference period," namely a period of time, such as the period between entry into the contract and closing. For simplicity, this book refers mostly to reference points.

2.58   If no reference point is stated in a representation, then in effect the reference point is when the representation is made.[38]

That would be on entry into the contract and at closing, if, as recommended, you use example [1] as your representations lead-in. (See 2.2.) But if you include a reference point in a representation, that representation would be concerned only with accuracy of facts at that the reference point, regardless of when the representation is made.

Matters Under the Seller's Control

2.59   Whether to include a reference point depends on the representation. Consider first a representation involving matters that are under the seller's control and that occur in the ordinary course of business, such as the contracts that the seller has entered into. (Assume that the seller routinely enters into contracts.) If no date is stated, then in effect the reference point is when the representation is made. Consequently, if the seller enters into a contract that includes the representation in [2] as well as the recommended representations lead-in (example [1]) and before closing enters into additional contracts, then at closing the representation in [2] would be inaccurate.

TABLE 2: THE REFERENCE POINT

[2]	Schedule 4.8 lists each contract to which the Seller is party.
[2a]	Schedule 4.8 lists each contract to which the Seller is party on the date of this agreement.

[2b]	✗	Schedule 4.8 lists each contract to which the Seller is party on the date of this agreement and at Closing.
[3]		The Seller is in compliance with all Laws.
[3a]	✗	On the date of this agreement, the Seller is in compliance with all Laws.
[4]		No litigation is pending against the Seller.
[4a]		On the date of this agreement, no litigation is pending against the Seller.
[4b]	✗	On the date of this agreement and at Closing, no litigation is pending against the Seller.

2.60   The prospect of that likely inaccuracy would present the seller with a potentially uncomfortable choice on entry into the contract: it could curtail its business operations by not entering into any additional contracts or it could enter into additional contracts and face the risk of the buyer's using the inaccurate representation to walk away from the deal or seek indemnification, or both. The buyer might be constrained by the implied duty of good faith,[39] but that would provide the seller limited comfort.

2.61 The seller could get out of this bind by having the buyer allow the seller to make instead the representation in [2a], which would serve to make the date of the agreement the reference point. In response, the buyer could address preclosing change in the matters covered by the representation by putting limits on the seller's preclosing operations.

2.62 For example, the buyer could insist that the contract provide that the seller must obtain the buyer's written consent to enter into any new contract before closing. But that wouldn't give the seller any more leeway when entering into contracts than would having the seller give the representation in [2]—even if [2] doesn't contain a reference point, the buyer could always agree to waive the representation inaccuracy that would result from the seller's entering into one or more additional contracts. And it could be just as restrictive—except to the extent that it's constrained by the implied duty of good faith, the buyer could simply refuse to give its consent. So the seller would be justified in countering that it should have to seek the buyer's consent only if a new contract is not in the ordinary course of business, or that the buyer should not be able to unreasonably withhold its consent. (See figure 3.)

2.63 The more the subject matter of a representation relates to seller actions that are outside the ordinary course of business, the less likely it is that the buyer would be willing to let the seller use the date of the agreement as a reference point and thereby remove from the scope of the representation any adverse changes between the date of the agreement and closing.

2.64 For example, an inaccuracy in the representation in [3]—in other words, any failure by the seller to comply with any law—could not reasonably be considered to be something that could arise in the ordinary course of business between entry into the contract and closing. As a result, absent other considerations it would be odd for the buyer to agree to the seller's giving the representation in [3a]. (See figure 3.)

2.65 Alternative [2b] differs from [2] and [2a] in that it includes as reference points both the date of the agreement and the closing. Doing so serves no purpose, given that using the recommended form of representations lead-in allows you to achieve the same result more economically. (See 2.24–27.)

Matters Not Under the Seller's Control

2.66 Different considerations apply when the matters addressed in a representation are not under the seller's control, in that any change between signing and closing could not be addressed by means of an undertaking by the seller. In that situation, whether the buyer would agree to add the date of the agreement as a reference point would likely depend on the nature of the changes that might occur between entry into the contract and closing.

2.67 Consider the representation in [4]. If the seller's business is such that it can expect to be sporadically subject to lawsuits, the seller would likely object to giving that representation—it could reasonably claim that it would be inappropriate for it to be subject to the risk that the buyer would refuse to close, or would bring a claim for indemnification, because one or more ordinary-course lawsuits are filed against the seller between entry into the contract and closing.

2.68   If the buyer agrees to add the date of the agreement as the reference point, as in [4a], it could protect itself by making it a condition to closing that the seller not be subject to any litigation commenced between signing and closing. (See figure 3.) This would constitute a gap-closing condition. (See 4.12.) Although that would ensure that the buyer couldn't bring a claim for indemnification if one or more lawsuits were filed between signing and closing, the seller might nevertheless balk, on the grounds that the buyer shouldn't be able to walk because of insignificant lawsuits. One way to address this concern would be to add a "material adverse change" qualification to that condition (see 2.92) or to have the condition exclude lawsuits in which the amount at issue is less than a stated dollar amount.

2.69   Of course, instead of adding that condition, the parties could agree to so qualify the representation (see 2.75), but the buyer would likely consider that the seller should be willing to give an unqualified representation regarding litigation pending on the date of the agreement.

FIGURE 3: ADDING REFERENCE POINTS AND QUALIFICATIONS TO REPRESENTATIONS

Shading indicates contract language; the unshaded text represents analysis.

Seller Representations	Analysis
Schedule 4.8 lists each contract to which the Seller is party.	This representation is unqualified. See 2.75. Omitting some or all qualifications relating to significance, making satisfaction of the buyer's bringdown condition subject to a materiality qualification, and making the seller's indemnification obligations subject to a basket is an alternative to including numerous materiality qualifications in the seller's representations; see 2.111.
Schedule 4.8 lists each contract to which the Seller is party *on the date of this agreement.*	If the seller enters into contracts in the ordinary course of business, the buyer might well agree to this qualification—adding the date of the agreement as a reference point. But it would make sense for the buyer to require, in exchange, that the following preclosing obligation be imposed on the seller, as it would give the buyer a measure of control over preclosing change: Without the prior written consent of the Buyer, [which the Buyer shall not unreasonably withhold,] the Seller shall not enter into any contract [other than in the ordinary course of business]. See 2.59–62.
Schedule 4.8 lists each *Material* contract to which the Seller is party.	Adding an appropriate qualification allows you to limit the scope of a representation to those matters that achieve the specified level of significance. It's standard for that to be accomplished by using the word *material.* Using *material* as a defined term would allow you to avoid the ambiguity otherwise associated with the word. See 2.76–85. This qualification using *Material* couldn't be reworded as a qualification using the phrase *material adverse change,* or MAC. See 2.97. The buyer might want any significance qualification to be disregarded in determining whether a basket has been "filled." See 5.24–27.
Schedule 4.8 lists each contract to which the Seller is party, *except for any contract for purchase of widgets that does not require the Seller to pay more than $X in the aggregate.*	This exception is an example of a bright-line alternative to using the word *material.* See 2.109.
To the Seller's Knowledge, Schedule 4.8 lists each contract to which the Seller is party	It would be unusual for the buyer to agree to this qualification, as the seller should know what contracts it's party to. See 2.113–116.
No litigation is pending against the Seller.	This representation is unqualified; see 2.75. Omitting some or all qualifications relating to significance, making satisfaction of the buyer's bringdown condition subject to a materiality qualification, and making the seller's indemnification obligations subject to a basket is an alternative to including numerous materiality qualifications in the seller's representations; see 2.111.
On the date of this agreement, no litigation is pending against the Seller.	If the seller's business is such that it can expect to be sporadically subject to lawsuits, the buyer might well agree to this qualification—adding the date of the agreement as a reference point. But it would make sense for the buyer to require, in exchange, that the following be added as a gap-closing condition to the buyer's obligation to close: that no litigation has been commenced against the Seller after the date of this agreement, [except for any litigation that would not reasonably be expected to result in a MAC] [except for any litigation in which the amount at issue is less than $X]. See 2.66–69.

FIGURE 3: ADDING REFERENCE POINTS AND QUALIFICATIONS TO REPRESENTATIONS (continued)

Seller Representations	Analysis
No *Material* litigation is pending against the Seller.	Adding an appropriate qualification allows you to limit the scope of a representation to those matters that achieve the specified level of significance. It's standard for that to be accomplished by using the word *material*. Using it as a defined term would allow you to avoid the ambiguity otherwise associated with *material*; see 2.76–85. This qualification using *Material* couldn't be reworded as a qualification using MAC. See 2.97. The buyer might want any significance qualification to be disregarded in determining whether a basket has been "filled." See 5.24–27.
No litigation is pending against the Seller, *except for any litigation that would not reasonably be expected to result in a MAC.*	If the buyer is concerned that an inaccuracy in that representation could adversely affect the fortunes of the seller, then it would be clearer to qualify that representation using MAC rather than just *Material*. But not all qualifications using *material* can be converted into MAC qualifications. See 2.96-97.
To the Seller's Knowledge, no litigation is pending against the Seller.	It would be unusual for the buyer to agree to this qualification, as the seller should know what litigation is pending against it. See 2.113-116. But a knowledge qualification is standard in representations regarding threatened litigation.
The Seller is in compliance with all laws.	This representation is unqualified; see 2.75. Omitting some or all qualifications relating to significance, making satisfaction of the buyer's bringdown condition subject to a materiality qualification, and making the seller's indemnification obligations subject to a basket is an alternative to including numerous materiality qualifications in the seller's representations; see 2.111.
As of the date of this agreement, the Seller is in compliance with all laws.	It would be unusual for the buyer to agree to this modification, as any failure by the seller to comply with any law could not reasonably be considered to be something that could arise in the ordinary course of business between entry into the contract and closing. See 2.63-64.
The Seller is in *Material* compliance with all laws.	If a representation contains two nouns that could be modified by *Material*, it would make most sense to modify the noun that represents the focus of the representation. In this case, the focus is compliance, not the laws themselves. See 2.90-91. The buyer might want any significance qualification to be disregarded in determining whether a basket has been "filled." See 5.24-27.
The Seller is in compliance with all laws, *except for any instances of noncompliance that would not reasonably be expected to result in a MAC.*	If the buyer is concerned whether a representation inaccuracy could have an adverse effect on the fortunes of the seller, then it would be clearer to qualify that representation by using MAC rather than *Material*. See 2.96. The buyer might want any significance qualification to be disregarded in determining whether a basket has been "filled." See 5.24-27.
To the Seller's Knowledge, the Seller is in compliance with all laws.	It would be unusual for the buyer to agree to this qualification, as the seller is in a better position to know whether it's in compliance with laws, and the buyer would likely argue that the seller should bear the risk of the unknown. See 2.113-116.
To the Seller's Knowledge, the Seller is not in violation of any Environmental Laws.	If the buyer agrees to this knowledge qualification, it would be appropriate for the buyer and the seller to address, in the definition of *Knowledge*, whose knowledge would be relevant and whether those one or more persons are subject to a duty to investigate. See 2.120-123.

2.70   Like [2b], example [4b] includes as reference
             points both the date of the agreement and
             the closing. And as with
             [2b] (see 2.65), that formula serves no
             purpose.

EXCEPTIONS

2.71   Unless a representation asserts absence of
             relevant information, as in [5], you have a
             choice of whether to present information
             within the core representation, as in [5a],
             or by means of an exception to the core
             representation, as in [5b] and [5c]. (To state
             an exception, you don't necessarily need to
             use the word *except*.) Information is usually
             presented as an exception if that which is
             being described is undesirable or present in
             limited quantities.

TABLE 3: EXCEPTIONS

[5]	The Seller is not subject to any pending Litigation.
[5a]	The only pending Litigation to which the Seller is subject is the Widgetco Lawsuit.
[5b]	The Seller is not subject to any Litigation other than the Widgetco Lawsuit.
[5c]	Except as stated in schedule 4.8, the Seller is not subject to any Litigation.

2.72   In [5b], the information constituting
             the exception is stated as part of the
             representation, but often an exception will

refer to items listed in a disclosure schedule, as in [5c].[40] (In addition to containing exceptions, schedules are used to present any factual information that supplements representations.) Schedules can be lettered or numbered consecutively, but once there are several of them, for ease of reference it's preferable to give each schedule the number of the section to which it relates.

2.73   If the information is voluminous, is being compiled by someone other than the party responsible for drafting the contract, or is being prepared according to a different timetable than the contract, it makes things easier for the drafter and the reader to present it in a schedule.

2.74   If the information is sensitive, it can be put in a set of schedules with a view to minimizing the risk of wider disclosure: when a contract is attached to a proxy statement or other disclosure document or is filed with the Securities and Exchange Commission, the filer can elect to omit the schedules to that contract.[41] But depending on the circumstances, that practice might violate securities laws.

QUALIFICATIONS RELATING TO SIGNIFICANCE

2.75   A drafter can elect to have any given representation be "qualified" so as to limit its scope. A representation can contain a qualification excluding those matters that don't achieve a specified level of significance, a knowledge qualification, or both. Any representation that contains no qualifications—[5] is an example of such a representation—is described as "unqualified" or "flat." (Conditions too can include qualifications regarding significance. See 4.25, 4.42.) Some of the issues discussed in this section are illustrated in figure 3.

The Problem with "Material"

2.76 Let's consider first excluding from the scope of a representation those matters that don't achieve a specified level of significance. It's standard for that to be accomplished using the word *material*.[42] It's a vague word, in that it provides for the possibility of borderline cases—some circumstances will clearly achieve the required significance, others clearly will not, and still others will fall in between, creating uncertainty. But it's also ambiguous, in that it conveys two different meanings.[43]

2.77 One meaning is "of such a nature that knowledge of the item would affect a person's decision-making process." (In this book, this meaning is referred to as the "affects a decision" meaning.) This meaning has been embraced in cases addressing securities laws violations, suppression of evidence in criminal matters, and a variety of other fields, as well as in Delaware Court of Chancery opinions on materiality in an M&A context, including *IBP, Inc. v. Tyson Foods, Inc.*[44] The Delaware cases concern the meaning of the phrase *material adverse change*, or MAC (see 2.88), but the level of significance applied to *material* in the context of MAC provisions should apply equally to use of the word *material* on its own.

2.78   In an M&A context, and from the buyer's perspective, this meaning of *material* refers to information that would have caused the buyer not to enter into the contract or would cause the buyer not to want to close the transaction. The standard is a high one.[45]

2.79   Another meaning is "significant"—in other words, "important enough to merit attention." This meaning would encompass a broader range of significance than the "affects a decision" meaning—for something to be material to a contract party, it would simply have to be of more than trivial significance.

2.80   In any given provision, such as the representation *Acme's financial records contain no material inaccuracies,* either meaning could conceivably be intended. In other words, *material* is ambiguous. (But that isn't the case with *material* when used in the phrase *material adverse change.* See 2.77, 2.93.)

2.81   This ambiguity could result in confusion. For example, a buyer and its counsel might assume that any nontrivial nondisclosure with respect to a given representation containing a qualification using *material* would be sufficient to render the representation inaccurate. By contrast, a court could well hold that for purposes of that representation, *material* conveys the "affects a decision" meaning. That could result in the buyer's not being entitled to be indemnified for any nondisclosure unless it were to meet the higher standard associated with that meaning.

2.82   Perhaps the simplest form of protection against this ambiguity would be to (1) use *material* to express only the "affects a decision" meaning, as that's the meaning that a court would likely attribute to the word, and (2) use bright-line alternatives to express the lesser level of significance. (See 2.109.)

2.83   But if in any given contract you wish to express both levels of significance, or you wish to express the lesser level of significance, it would be safest to use two different terms for the two meanings. This book recommends that you use *material* to convey the "affects a decision" meaning and use *significant* to convey a broader range of significance. Because that's not how qualifications relating to significance are currently handled, this recommendation represents something of a trial balloon.

2.84   But there's precedent for this proposed distinction: in connection with guidance on evaluating internal controls, the Securities and Exchange Commission has defined the term "significant deficiency" to mean a deficiency "that is less severe than a material weakness, yet important enough to merit attention by those responsible for oversight of the registrant's financial reporting."[46]

Defining "Material"

2.85   If you wish to use *material* to convey the "affects a decision" meaning, you should make that meaning explicit, so as to purge *material* of its ambiguity. In so doing, you'd need to make clear whose perspective applies for purposes of determining materiality. In *IBP, Inc. v. Tyson Foods, Inc.*, the court considered materiality from the perspective of the "reasonable acquiror"; for this approach to apply in any context, one would need to refer to the perspective of a reasonable person in the position of the party in question.

2.86   To incorporate these concepts into the meaning of *material*, it would be best to use it as a defined term. (That's not the current practice—the author has determined that none of the contracts in the 2009 Private Target Deal Points Study (see "Preface—Features of this Book") offers a lexical definition of *material*.) You might find it useful also to define *materially*—for one thing, as a matter of logic it's the most appropriate choice for use in the bringdown condition. (See 4.25.) The exact definition would depend on the context and on which parties are covered by the definition. In an M&A context, the following definition would be appropriate as a definition relating to the buyer:

> **"Material"** and **"Materially"** refer to a level of significance that would have affected any decision of a reasonable person in the Buyer's position regarding whether to enter into this agreement or would affect any decision of a reasonable person in the Buyer's position regarding whether to consummate the transaction contemplated by this agreement.

2.87   By referring to entry into the agreement and consummation of the transaction, the definition would address circumstances relating to the periods before and after the date of the agreement.

2.88   It's commonplace for both the seller and the buyer to be subject to provisions containing a materiality qualification. For example, if the bringdown condition to the buyer's obligations is subject to a materiality qualification, often the bringdown condition to the seller's obligations will be subject to a materiality qualification too. (See 4.26.) In such contexts, the definition of *Material* and *Materially* would need to apply to all parties:

> **"Material"** and **"Materially"** refer, with respect to a given Person, to a level of significance that would have affected any decision of a reasonable person in that Person's position regarding whether to enter into this agreement or would affect any decision of a reasonable person in that Person's position regarding whether to consummate the transaction contemplated by this agreement.

2.89   If you use that definition, each bringdown condition would need to make it clear from whose perspective materiality is determined. (See 4.26.)

Using "Material"

2.90   A representation might contain only one noun that could be modified by *Material*, as in [6]. But often a representation

45

contains two such nouns, raising the question whether, for purposes of adding a materiality qualification to the representation, you should modify one or the other noun, as in [7] and [7a], or both, as in [7b]. It would make the most sense to modify the noun that represents the focus of the representation. The focus of [7] and its variations is contract defaults, not the contracts themselves, so it would make the most sense to have *Material* modify *default*, as in [7].

TABLE 4: USING "MATERIAL"

[6]		Schedule 4.8 lists each Material contract to which the Seller is party.
[7]	✓	The Seller is not in Material default under any contract to which it is party.
[7a]		The Seller is not in default under any Material contract to which it is party.
[7b]		The Seller is not in Material default under any Material contract to which it is party.

2.91 By contrast, [7a] would seem both overinclusive and underinclusive—it would be rendered inaccurate by any default under any of the contracts in question, no matter how trivial, but wouldn't be rendered inaccurate by default under a contract that doesn't meet the high level of significance inherent in *Material*, no matter how serious the consequences of that default. And [7b] would be underinclusive—it would seem illogical to exclude from the scope of the representation, just because they involve contracts other than Material contracts, defaults that would otherwise fall within the definition of *Material*.

Using "Material Adverse Change"

2.92   The word *material* is commonly used in the phrase *material adverse change*, or MAC. MAC is preferable to the term *material adverse effect*, as unlike that term MAC works equally well in all contexts.[47] It's potentially confusing to use both MAC and *material adverse effect* in a contract, and generally it should be unnecessary to do so.[48]

2.93   MAC is used to refer to a material adverse change in a party's fortunes, and for the sake of convenience and consistency MAC is generally used as a defined term. Courts and practitioners appear to accept that when used in MAC, *material* conveys the "affects a decision" meaning—any party invoking a MAC provision would need to make a strong showing. (See 2.77–78.)

2.94   In representations, MAC is used in two ways. First, the seller can make a representation regarding nonoccurrence of a MAC since a given date, as in *Since December 31, 2009, no MAC has occurred.* Because it encompasses the possibility of future MACs, the following version would be more favorable to the buyer: *Since December 31, 2009, there has not occurred any MAC or any event or circumstance that would reasonably be expected to result in a MAC.*

2.95   Second, a MAC provision can be used instead of just *material* to add a materiality qualification to a representation. For example, an alternative to *Acme's financial records contain no Material inaccuracies* would be *Acme's financial records contain no inaccuracies other than inaccuracies that would not reasonably be expected to result in a MAC.*

2.96   Whether to use MAC or just *Material* to qualify a representation depends on what significance is being measured. If the buyer is concerned that an inaccuracy in that representation could adversely affect the fortunes of the seller, then it would be clearer to qualify that representation using MAC rather than just *Material,* even though a court might construe *Material* by itself as conveying the same meaning in this context. But if the buyer is instead concerned about a potential inaccuracy directly affecting the buyer—if, for instance, the representation concerns assets of the seller that are of little significance to the seller but are central to the buyer's plans—it would make sense to stick with *material.*

2.97   But not all qualifications using *material* can be converted into qualifications using MAC. For example, [6] and [7a] cannot reworded using MAC, whereas [7] can be revised using MAC to read as follow: *The Seller is not in default under any contract to which it is party, except for any default that would not reasonably be expected to result in a MAC.*

Defining "Material Adverse Change"

2.98   Regarding how you define MAC, this book recommends that you use the following core definition:

> **"Material Adverse Change"** means any Material adverse change in the business, results of operations, assets, liabilities, or financial condition of the Seller.

2.99   Explaining what is included in and excluded from this definition and its various permutations is beyond the scope of this book.[49] But note that much of any negotiations regarding how to define MAC would likely revolve around carve-outs from the definition.

2.100   Note also that in this definition, what needs to experience a material adverse change in order for a MAC to occur—in other words, the "field of change"—doesn't include *prospects*.

2.101   Including *prospects* is a recurring bone of contention. The buyer wants it in—the future of the business, it says, is a legitimate concern, given that the buyer is acquiring the business so as to operate it in the future. The seller wants it excluded—it is willing, it says, to stand behind how the business is currently being operated, but future operations are the buyer's concern. More often than not, the seller wins this battle.[50]

2.102   But if the seller's representation regarding nonoccurrence of a MAC includes the phrase *or any event or circumstance that would reasonably be expected to result in a MAC,* and if MAC qualifications in the seller's representations are phrased using the formula *would* [or *would not*] *reasonably be expected to result in a MAC,* that would afford the buyer protection comparable to that afforded by *prospects* while making less likely the kind of skirmish that parties commonly engage in over whether to include *prospects* in the field of change. This approach has been referred to as incorporating *prospects* by the "back door."

"Significant"

2.103 As for using *significant* to convey the "important enough to merit attention" meaning of *material,* it would be best to make it explicit that the broader meaning is intended, and the best way to do that would be to use *significant* as a defined term, as in *Acme's financial records contain no Significant inaccuracies.* This book recommends that you define *significant* as follows:

> **"Significant"** means important enough, from the perspective of a reasonable person in the Buyer's position, to merit attention, and it includes a lesser level of significance than does the defined term "Material."

2.104 Through contrast with the definition of *Material,* this definition specifies that in a relative sense the broader meaning is intended. And it does so in an absolute sense, too, by offering "important enough to merit attention" as the lexical definition of *significant.*

2.105 As does the definition of *Material* (see 2.85), this definition of *Significant* addresses the issue of whose perspective applies for purposes of determining whether something is trivial.

Using Qualifications Relating to Significance

2.106 A buyer that wishes to close a transaction without delay may be particularly amenable to having a given representation be subject to a qualification using *Material* or *Significant* if the alternative would be having the seller devote an inordinate amount of time to compiling a schedule of exceptions. Beyond that, whether to make a representation (or a condition) subject to such a qualification is essentially a function of the respective bargaining power of the parties.[51]

2.107 That said, certain representations are rarely subject to qualifications relating to significance, either because they are too straightforward to be anything other than unqualified or because the matters being represented are sufficiently fundamental that the buyer doesn't want to countenance any inaccuracies. Such representations include representations as to organization, capitalization, and authority to enter into the transaction.[52]

Limiting Significance Qualifications

2.108 Of the two standards, qualifications using *Significant* seem the less useful. Determining whether a given issue merits the buyer's attention is prone to arbitrariness, given the low threshold involved. And any party could reasonably claim that if it's willing to go to court to recover damages that it claims arose from inaccuracy of a representation subject to a qualifications using *Significant*, then by definition the inaccuracy was nontrivial.

2.109 So you might want to avail yourself of bright-line alternatives. Instead of having a party make a representation as to absence of *breach of any Significant contract to which the Seller is party,* you could instead refer to absence of *breach of any contract to which the Seller is party that is listed on schedule 2.4.* And rather than having a party make a representation as to absence of *any pending Significant litigation,* you might want to refer to absence of litigation involving an amount in excess of a stated dollar amount or seeking injunctive relief.

2.110 And in some contexts you might decide to dispense with a qualification using *Significant* and do without any substitute.

Relation to the Bringdown Condition and Indemnification

2.111 More generally, the seller might be willing to omit from its representations some or all qualifications relating to significance— whether using *Material, Significant,* or more precise alternatives—if you incorporate a materiality qualification in the buyer's bringdown condition, using *Materially* (see 4.25), and make any seller indemnification obligations subject to a basket (see 5.23). Doing so should eliminate any concern on the part of the seller that giving an unqualified representation could result in the transaction not closing due to, or result in that party's incurring indemnification liability for, a relatively minor inaccuracy. (See figure 3.) You might want to apply this approach to both the seller and the buyer.

2.112 A seller might want to retain qualifications relating to significance in any representations that it expects would otherwise likely be inaccurate when made at closing, but it should be able instead to address that concern by negotiating an appropriate basket.

KNOWLEDGE QUALIFICATIONS

2.113 Another standard qualification used in representations is the knowledge qualification, as in *To the Seller's Knowledge, the Seller is not in violation of any Environmental Laws.* The effect of such a qualification is that the representing party is not representing as to absolute accuracy, but instead is representing that to that party's knowledge the statement of fact in question is accurate. Unlike qualifications relating to significance, knowledge qualifications have limited implications for other categories of provisions. For one instance of interplay with another category of provisions, see 4.38.

2.114 A party will want to include a knowledge qualification in a representation it makes if that party is not in a position to determine whether the representation is accurate, usually because the representation refers to matters that might be hidden (such as environmental contamination) or are under the control of others (such as threatened litigation).

2.115   Who bears the risk of unknown problems is a function of risk allocation.[53] The seller would likely argue that it would be unfair to insist that it make a representation if it has no way of knowing whether the representation is accurate. By contrast, the buyer would likely argue that as between the buyer and the seller, the seller should bear the risk of the unknown.

2.116   Certain representations—such as representations regarding threatened litigation—almost invariably include a knowledge limitation. Others—such as a company's representation as to its capitalization—never do, because they relate to matters over which the seller has control. In the case of yet others— such as representations as to violations of environmental laws—there is no fixed practice. If including a knowledge qualification in a given representation would not be the standard practice, getting the buyer to accept that qualification might require that the seller either have superior bargaining power or be willing to make concessions elsewhere in the contract.

2.117   In phrasing a knowledge qualification, don't refer to *the best of* someone's knowledge. For one thing, it adds nothing, because *to the best of Acme's knowledge* means exactly the same thing as *to Acme's knowledge*. Furthermore, using *the best of* could lead a reader to assume incorrectly that it implies an obligation to investigate (see 2.123) or some sort of heightened level of knowledge.[54]

2.118 Also, you should consider using *knowledge* as a defined term. Doing so would allow you to address two issues that otherwise would be subject to uncertainty: whose knowledge would be relevant and whether those one or more persons are under a duty to investigate.

2.119 If the term is to be used with respect to a single party, you would use the form of autonomous definition[55] in [8]. If it is to be used with respect to more than one party, you would define the term using the form of autonomous definition in [8a], which should be revised appropriately if the parties are all individuals or all legal entities.

TABLE 5: KNOWLEDGE QUALIFICATIONS

[8]   **"Seller's Knowledge"** means *[insert level of knowledge; see [10] and its variations]* of *[specify whose knowledge applies; see [9] and its variations]*.

[8a] **"Knowledge"** means, with respect to any Person, *[insert level of knowledge; see [10] and its variations]* of that Person (if that Person is an individual) or *[specify whose knowledge applies; see [9] and its variations]* (if that Person is not an individual).

[9]   John Doe

[9a] [the Seller's] [that Person's] executive officers [(as defined in rule 405 promulgated under the Securities Act)]

[9b] [the Seller's] [that Person's] directors and executive officers

[9c] [the Seller's] [that Person's] directors, officers, and any other persons having supervisory or management responsibilities with respect to [the Seller's] [that Person's] operations

[9d] directors and officers of [the Seller and any Seller Subsidiary] [that Person and any of its Subsidiaries] and any other person having supervisory or management responsibilities with respect to the operations of [the Seller or any Seller Subsidiary] [that Person or any of its Subsidiaries]

[9e] [the Seller's] [that Person's] shareholders, directors, officers, and other employees

[9f] the shareholders, directors, officers, and other employees of [the Seller and any Seller subsidiary] [that Person and any of its Subsidiaries]

[10] the actual knowledge, without any requirement to investigate,

[10a] the actual knowledge, after inquiry of [the Seller's employees] [that Person's employees] [employees of the Seller Plant],

[10b] the actual knowledge, after reasonable investigation,

2.120   If the seller is an entity rather than an individual, one is faced with the issue of whose knowledge would be relevant for purposes of determining the accuracy of a representation containing a knowledge qualification. The seller would want to limit the number of people whose knowledge would be relevant, whereas the buyer would want to specify as broad a group as possible. Example [9] and its variations demonstrate some of the possibilities, from limited to broader.

2.121   The reference in [9a] to rule 405 would serve to reduce the likelihood of disagreement as to who is an executive officer, but it should be used in a given contract only if any party benefiting from a knowledge qualification is a public company.

2.122   A company selling a subsidiary or division would face the question of whose knowledge is relevant for purposes of representations regarding the business being sold.[56] Managers of the business being sold would be the most knowledgeable, but the seller could well be concerned that if they remain with the business being sold, they might be pressured into determining that they had, in fact, known that a given representation was inaccurate, or may come to that conclusion themselves in their eagerness to ingratiate themselves with their new employer. Consequently, the seller might try to omit from the definition of *Knowledge* any officers involved in the business being sold, something the buyer would resist.

2.123 In addition to the question of whose knowledge is relevant, any definition of *Knowledge* should address whether it means actual knowledge or knowledge after some level of investigation. A more limited alternative to the reasonable-investigation standard stated in [10b] is a standard based on inquiry of a specified group of employees, as in [10a]. Avoid, as being unclear, references to *reasonable knowledge*.

2.124 Don't define *knowledge* to mean knowledge on a given date. In particular, defining it to mean knowledge on the date of the agreement would serve to render irrelevant any knowledge that's acquired after the date of the agreement. It would be functionally equivalent to inserting the date of the agreement as a reference point in all representations that are qualified by knowledge.[57] (See 2.56.)

REFERRING TO REPRESENTATION INACCURACIES

2.125 One breaches an obligation, but not a representation. Instead, a representation, like any statement of fact, is either accurate or inaccurate.[58] Observing this distinction might help drafters avoid inappropriately lumping representations with obligations, for example by providing for the possibility of cure of not only breached obligations but also "breached" representations—a party cannot subsequently make accurate an inaccurate representation. (See 2.9.)

■ CHAPTER 3

Preclosing Obligations

FUNCTION

3.1   Obligations can be found in different parts of an M&A contract—in the deal provisions, the indemnification provisions, even the boilerplate.

3.2   But in M&A contracts, it's standard practice to group together certain obligations in one or more articles. These obligations fall into two categories—preclosing obligations and postclosing obligations. Preclosing obligations in turn fall into two subcategories—obligations related to the transaction (referred to in this book as "transactional obligations") and obligations related to operation of the target business between signing and closing.

3.3   Such grouped obligations are often referred to as "covenants," but that's an unhelpful term. For one thing, there's no good reason to call obligations by another name just because they occur in a different part of a contract. And the word *covenant* has a quaint Old Testament (or *Raiders of the Lost Ark*) quality to it. So rather than giving the heading "Covenants" to an article containing obligations, use instead "Certain Obligations."

3.4   This book concerns itself with only transactional obligations—it is those obligations that raise issues relating to interplay of the categories of contract provisions.

3.5   In formulating transactional obligations for a given contract, a drafter should aim to be as economical as possible. This is accomplished by playing off of other categories of contract provisions.

THE ENSURE-THE-CONDITIONS-ARE-SATISFIED OBLIGATION

3.6   In this regard, the key transactional obligation is the seller's obligation to use reasonable efforts to ensure that the conditions benefiting the buyer have been satisfied. (See figure 4.) This book refers to this obligation as the "ensure-the-conditions-are-satisfied" obligation. (The seller would presumably want to impose a reciprocal obligation on the buyer.)

Using "Reasonable Efforts"

3.7   Because invariably one or more conditions benefitting the buyer won't be under the control of the seller (see 4.10), it's appropriate to use a *reasonable efforts* standard in the ensure-the-conditions-are-satisfied obligation.

3.8   Don't use instead *best efforts* or some other *efforts* variant.[59] Many practitioners are under the impression that an obligation to use best efforts to comply with an

60

FIGURE 4: SUBCATEGORIES OF TRANSACTIONAL OBLIGATIONS

Category	Transactional Obligations
Ensure-the-conditions-are-satisfied obligation	Subject to section __ [any Seller obligation to take one or more specified actions required to satisfy a particular condition], the Seller shall use reasonable efforts to cause to be satisfied the conditions stated in section __ [Conditions to the Buyer's Obligations] and section __ [any condition to the Seller's obligation that needs, or might benefit from, action by the Seller in order to be satisfied].
Ensure-the-representations-are-accurate obligation	The Seller shall use reasonable efforts to cause all the representations made by the Seller in article 2 to be accurate as of the Closing.
Obligation to use efforts to satisfy a specific condition	EXAMPLE: The Seller shall use reasonable efforts to obtain all Consents.
Obligation stating actions required to satisfy a specific condition	EXAMPLE: [Obligation stating steps the Seller is required to take to obtain shareholder approval or regulatory consents.]
Obligation to provide information on nonsatisfaction of conditions	The Seller shall promptly notify the Buyer of any event or circumstance as a result of which any of the conditions stated in section __ [Conditions to the Buyer's Obligations] could not or would not reasonably be expected to be satisfied.
Other transactional obligations	EXAMPLES: [Obligations requiring that the Seller— • give the Buyer access to the Seller premises and records • not disclose any confidential information of the Seller • not enter into any alternative transaction • sign any additional documents and take any additional actions necessary or desirable to consummate the transaction]

(vertical label left of table:) REBUNDANT

61

obligation is more exacting than an obligation to use reasonable efforts, but that notion has two serious flaws. First, in *best efforts* as the phrase is generally used, the word *best* provides a rhetorical flourish that doesn't affect meaning. And second, holding that *best efforts* requires a level of effort beyond *reasonable efforts* would in effect impose on a contract party under a best-efforts obligation the need to behave other than reasonably—in other words, unreasonably; and that party would be entitled to wonder exactly what level of unreasonable effort would be required to satisfy the obligation. That's an unworkable standard.

3.9 And adding the word *commercially* to *reasonable efforts* adds nothing—determining what is reasonable for purposes of a business contract necessarily requires that you take into account the commercial context.

3.10 So it comes as no surprise that U.S. caselaw overwhelmingly supports the notion that all *efforts* standards mean essentially the same thing—*reasonable efforts*.[60] Courts in England,[61] Australia,[62] and Canada[63] are more willing to see a distinction between *best efforts* and *reasonable efforts* (in the case of England, *best endeavours* and *reasonable endeavours*), but unsurprisingly they fail to articulate a coherent basis for such a distinction.

3.11 In sensitive contexts, you may want to use *reasonable efforts* as a defined term.[64] Here's the recommended core definition:

> **"Reasonable Efforts"** means,
> with respect to a given obligation, the
> efforts that a reasonable person in [the
> promisor's] [Acme's] position would
> use so as to perform that obligation as
> promptly as possible.

3.12   This core definition wouldn't be suitable
in all contexts. For example, if a party is
required to use reasonable efforts to prevent
something from happening, or to use
reasonable efforts to continue performing
an ongoing obligation, it wouldn't make
sense to refer to prompt performance of
that obligation.

3.13   As with the definition of MAC (see 2.99),
negotiations regarding the definition of
Reasonable Efforts would likely focus on
carve-outs.[65]

Implications

3.14   Consider what might occur if you were to
omit the ensure-the-conditions-are-satisfied
obligation: The seller has represented
that it needs to obtain certain consents to
close the deal, and it's a condition to the
buyer's obligation to close that the seller
have obtained those consents. If the seller
isn't obligated to use reasonable efforts
to obtain those consents, it could elect to
sit on its hands, leaving the buyer with
an unpalatable choice—either not closing
or assuming any costs that arise from the
seller's failure to obtain the consents. It's not
clear that the buyer could sue the seller and
win—even if a court were to read into the
contract a requirement that the seller act in

good faith, that could well be a less exacting standard than that imposed by an ensure-the-conditions-are-satisfied obligation.[66]

3.15 It might be that satisfaction of any one or more conditions to the *seller's* obligations needs, or might benefit from, action by the seller to be satisfied. If those conditions aren't included among the conditions to the buyer's obligations, you should ensure that those seller's conditions are covered by the seller's ensure-the-conditions-are-satisfied obligation. (See figure 4.) An example of such a seller condition is a condition that the seller have closed another unrelated transaction.

Redundancy

3.16 When you impose on the seller an ensure-the-conditions-are-satisfied obligation, it would be redundant to require that the seller also make reasonable efforts to ensure that its representations are accurate. (See figure 4.) That would be covered by the ensure-the-conditions-are-satisfied obligation, assuming that the conditions to the buyer's obligations include a bringdown condition, which should be the case. (See 4.25.) Nevertheless, one sees contracts that include both of those transactional obligations.

3.17 It would also be redundant to include along with the ensure-the-conditions-are-satisfied obligation any provisions imposing on the seller an obligation to use reasonable efforts to satisfy a given condition, in that any such obligation would be subsumed within the ensure-the-conditions-are-satisfied obligation. For example, it would be redundant to include an obligation that the seller use reasonable efforts to obtain necessary consents. (See figure 4.) Nevertheless, such obligations are commonplace in contracts containing an ensure-the-conditions-are-satisfied obligation.

OBLIGATION STATING ACTIONS TO TAKE TO SATISFY A CONDITION

3.18   But it wouldn't be redundant for the buyer to impose on the seller an obligation to take specified actions aimed at satisfying a given condition (rather than just using reasonable efforts), even if the contract imposes on the seller an ensure-the-conditions-are-satisfied obligation. (See figure 4.) An example of such an obligation would be one that specifies actions the seller must take in connection with securing shareholder approval.[67] Another example would be an obligation specifying filings that the seller must make to secure regulatory approvals. Make the ensure-the-conditions-are-satisfied obligation subject to any obligation to take specified steps to satisfy a condition (see figure 4): the reasonable-efforts standard of the former would be trumped by the absolute standard of the latter.

OBLIGATION TO PROVIDE INFORMATION ON NONSATISFACTION OF CONDITIONS

3.19   It stands to reason that the buyer would rather be informed promptly of any actual or potential inaccuracies in the seller's representations, or any breach or potential breach of the seller's obligations, instead of waiting until closing, or afterwards, to find out. This can be accomplished by requiring the seller to notify the buyer promptly of any event or circumstance that would preclude, or would reasonably be expected to preclude, satisfaction of one or more conditions to the buyer's obligations (see figure 4). An indemnification-even-if-you-know provision would make it clear that any such notice would have no effect on the buyer's ability to seek indemnification for inaccuracies in any seller representations. (See 5.12.)

3.20   In many contracts, the issue of the seller's preclosing disclosure of inaccuracies is addressed by requiring the seller to update its disclosure schedules if any seller representation was inaccurate when made on the date of the agreement or would be inaccurate when made at closing. This approach has a number of drawbacks.[68]

3.21   First, from a drafting perspective, updating an inaccurate representation might require amending that representation in addition to, or instead of, updating any disclosure schedules. For instance, if a given representation doesn't provide for any scheduled exceptions, then fixing that inaccuracy by adding a schedule of exceptions would, strictly speaking, also require revising the representation to refer to that schedule.

3.22   Second, provisions regarding updating often require that the schedules be updated not only to reflect inaccurate representations but also any failure by the seller to comply with any obligation and any event or circumstance that would prevent any condition to the buyer's obligations from being satisfied. Updating schedules to reflect the latter two categories of information would require schedules to perform something other than their intended function—stating factual information that supplements, or constitutes an exception to, a set of representations. (See 2.72.)

3.23 Third, although it could be argued that such provisions allow schedules to be updated to take into account ordinary-course changes, such as the seller's entering into contracts between the date of the agreement and closing, the better way to provide for such changes would be to include the date of the agreement as a reference point in the representations in question and to address preclosing change in either a preclosing obligation (if the change is under the seller's control) or a condition (if it isn't under the seller's control). (See 2.56–70.)

3.24 And fourth, provisions that address the seller's updating of schedules usually go on to state that updating the schedules serves merely to inform the buyer and has no effect on closing conditions or the seller's indemnification obligations. (Such language has broadly the same effect as "indemnification-even-if-you-know" provisions. (See 5.12.) It would be simpler instead to incorporate the concept of updating in a way that leaves the schedules unaffected.

OTHER TRANSACTIONAL OBLIGATIONS

3.25   Other seller transactional obligations
don't relate to satisfaction of conditions.
Instead, they require the seller to take steps
to facilitate the transaction and otherwise
protect the buyer's interests. (See figure 4.)

■ CHAPTER 4

Conditions

FUNCTION

4.1 In a contract that provides for a deferred closing, the conditions state what has to happen before the parties will be required to consummate the transaction. Usually a contract will contain a set of conditions for each side, but conditions that apply to both sides can be grouped together into a third set of conditions, thereby avoiding repetition. Whether it's worthwhile to do so depends on how many such conditions there are.

THE CONDITIONS LEAD-IN

4.2 As with representations, any set of conditions will have a lead-in. This book recommends that you use [11] as your form of conditions lead-in.

TABLE 6: THE CONDITIONS LEAD-IN

[11]	✓	The Buyer's obligation to consummate the transaction contemplated by this agreement is subject to satisfaction of the following conditions:
[11a]	✗	The Buyer's obligation ... is subject to satisfaction of the following conditions [*on or before the Closing*]:

[11b]   ✖   The Buyer's obligation ... is subject to satisfaction [*or waiver by the Buyer at any time in its sole discretion to the extent permitted by applicable law*] of the following conditions:

[11c]   ✖   The Buyer's obligation ... is subject to satisfaction of the following conditions [*, each of which is for the Buyer's sole benefit*]:

4.3   Like the representations lead-in, the conditions lead-in often suffers from bloat. In [11a], [11b], and [11c], the superfluous language is in italics and in brackets.

4.4   Example [11a] exhibits circularity: If the conditions are satisfied and the transaction closes, then the conditions necessarily will have been satisfied on or before the closing. The closing is a function of satisfaction of the conditions rather than an independent timing constraint.

4.5   The waiver language in [11b] is unnecessary. The buyer may waive any condition regardless of whether the contract says so, unless by law that condition cannot be waived.[69] Receipt of shareholder approval that is required by statute is an example of a condition that cannot be waived.[70]

4.6   And because it's self-evident, nothing would be gained by specifying, as in [11c], that any condition to the buyer's obligation may be invoked only by the buyer.[71]

"CONDITION PRECEDENT" AND "CONDITION SUBSEQUENT"

4.7   Using in a contract the phrase *condition precedent* rather than simply *condition* adds nothing other than a whiff of pedanticism. And avoid the phrase *condition subsequent*—a condition subsequent is something that, if it occurs, will bring something else to an end.[72] It's much clearer to say instead that if X happens, Y will terminate.

4.8   If you need any encouragement to dispense with these terms, note that the Restatement (Second) of Contracts has already done so.[73]

CATEGORIES

4.9   Conditions to closing can be divided by function into three categories: gating conditions, maintain-the-bargain conditions, and transactional conditions. (This terminology is new.) See figure 5 for examples of each category. Instead of exhibiting the deficient grammar and structure that generally afflict closing conditions, these examples don't use *shall* and are structured as *that*-clauses.[74]

4.10   Gating conditions relate to whatever caused the parties to provide for a deferred closing—usually the need to secure the consent of shareholders, a government body, or a party to some other contract (such as a landlord under a lease), or the need to first consummate another transaction, such as a financing. Gating conditions to the buyer's obligation to close could relate to consents needed by, or transactions to be entered into by, the buyer, the seller, or both.

4.11   Maintain-the-bargain conditions are geared to ensuring that nothing untoward—from the perspective of the party that has the benefit of those conditions—has happened between the date of the agreement and closing. This kind of condition can be broken down into four subcategories: the bringdown condition, the compliance-with-obligations condition, gap-closing conditions, and external conditions.

4.12   The bringdown condition and compliance-with-obligations condition are discussed below. (See 4.17–42.) Gap-closing conditions are conditions that address the gap in coverage when a representation regarding something that isn't under the seller's control speaks only as of the date of signing, due to use of the date of the agreement as a reference point in the representation. (See 2.68.) And external conditions relate to economic or other circumstances readily ascertainable by the buyer. (Other than "bringdown condition," this terminology too is new.)

4.13   A transactional condition relates to items that a party is to deliver at closing. Delivery of closing items can be stated instead, or even in addition, as an obligation, but that has two shortcomings. First, some of the items to be delivered, such as legal opinions, are not entirely within a party's control. And second, delivery of closing items is best understood as a condition, as it doesn't constitute an end unto itself but instead serves to give the other party sufficient comfort to close. If the seller is subject to an ensure-the-conditions-are-satisfied obligation, refusing to supply the

FIGURE 5: CATEGORIES OF CONDITIONS

Lead-in: The Buyer's obligation to consummate the transaction contemplated by this agreement is subject to satisfaction of the following conditions:

Related Representation	Category		Conditions to the Buyer's Obligation to Close
	Gating conditions		EXAMPLE: that the waiting period under the Hart-Scott-Rodino Act has expired or been terminated;
			EXAMPLE: that the Seller's shareholders have authorized the Seller to enter into this agreement and consummate the transactions contemplated by this agreement;
			EXAMPLE: that the Seller has obtained all [Material] Consents;
			EXAMPLE: that the Buyer has received the proceeds of the Financing;
Between January 1, 2011, and the date of this agreement, no MAC has occurred	Bringdown condition	Maintain-the-bargain conditions	that [individually and in the aggregate,] the representations made by the Seller in article __ [Seller's Representations] were [Materially] accurate on the date of this agreement and are [Materially] accurate at Closing;
	Compliance-with-obligations condition		that the Seller has [Materially] complied [, individually and in the aggregate,] with those of its obligations under this agreement that it is required to comply with before the Closing;
	Gap-closing conditions		EXAMPLE: that no MAC has occurred since the date of this agreement;
	External conditions		that no Proceedings are pending that seek to prevent consummation of the Transaction;
			that there is in effect no Law or Order that prevents consummation of the Transaction;
			EXAMPLE: that the market price of the Seller's common stock is at least $23.00;
	Transactional conditions		EXAMPLE: that the Seller has delivered to the Buyer the following items:
			EXAMPLE: that the Buyer has receive from the Seller's counsel an opinion dated the Closing Date in the form of exhibit __;

required items would subject the seller to a claim for indemnification. (See 3.6.)

4.14 Some drafters lump together in an article entitled "Closing" a section stating when and where the closing is to be held and a section stating that the parties are obligated to deliver the listed items at closing. If delivery of closing items is treated as a condition rather than an obligation, what remains is hardly worth a separate article—the section addressing the "where" and "when" of closing could more conveniently be included in the deal provisions.[75]

4.15 If a topic is covered in a representation or an obligation, generally it would be redundant to address it in a condition as well. (See 1.7.) But seller representations cover only matters that pertain to the seller; for purposes of a condition, a buyer may want to include matters pertaining to the buyer.

4.16 Consider for example the standard seller representation that no litigation seeking to block the transaction is pending against it. In a contract that contains such a representation, nothing would be accomplished by making it a condition to the buyer's obligations that no such litigation is pending—through the bringdown condition, any inaccuracy in the representation would, subject to any materiality qualification in the bringdown condition, give the buyer grounds not to close. But relying on the bringdown condition wouldn't give the buyer grounds for not closing if the *buyer*, as opposed to the seller, were subject to litigation that seeks to block the transaction. That's why the buyer should want to have any such litigation form the basis of an external condition to the buyer's obligation to close. (See figure 5.)

THE BRINGDOWN CONDITION

4.17   A bringdown condition allows one side to use inaccuracy in the other side's representations to relieve it of its obligation to close. This book recommends that the basic form of bringdown condition read as stated in [12]. "Bringdown condition" is an accepted term of art, but it's something of a misnomer. If you use the recommended form of lead-in—namely example [1]— the seller would in effect be making its representations on both the date of the agreement and the closing, so there would be nothing to "bring down" to closing.

TABLE 7: THE BRINGDOWN CONDITION

[12]   ✓   that the representations made by the Seller in article 2 were accurate on the date of this agreement and are accurate at Closing;

[12a]   that the representations made by the Seller in article 2 are accurate at Closing;

[12b]   that individually and in the aggregate, the representations made by the Seller in article 2 were Materially accurate on the date of this agreement and are Materially accurate at Closing;

[12c]   that from the Buyer's perspective, individually and in the aggregate the representations made by the Seller in article 2 were Materially accurate on the date of this agreement and are Materially accurate at Closing;

[12d]   that each representation made by the Seller in article 2 was Materially accurate on the date of this agreement and is Materially accurate at Closing;

[12e] ✘ that except for any inaccuracies that would not reasonably be expected to result in, individually or in the aggregate, a Material Adverse Change, the representations made by the Seller in article 2 were accurate on the date of this agreement and are accurate at Closing;

[12f] ✘ that in all respects (in the case of any representation containing any materiality qualification) or in all material respects (in the case of any representation that does not contain any materiality qualification), the representations made by the Seller were accurate on the date of this agreement and are accurate at Closing;

[12g] ✘ that the representations made by the Seller in article 2, disregarding all materiality qualifications, were accurate on the date of this agreement and are accurate at Closing, except for any inaccuracies that would not reasonably be expected to have a Material Adverse Change;

| [12h] | ✗ | that the representations made by the Seller in article 2 were accurate on the date of this agreement and are accurate at Closing (except to the extent those representations specifically speak as of a specified date); |

"Accurate"

4.18 In the bringdown condition it's standard to refer to representations as being *true and correct*. Use instead *accurate*, which avoids the legalistic redundancy of *true and correct*.

Relevance of When Representations Are Made

4.19 A representation made on the date of the agreement speak as of that date only, so a representation that's accurate on entry into the contract will necessarily be accurate at closing, and all other times too. (See 2.9.) So if the seller makes its representations only on the date of the agreement, then strictly speaking it would be redundant to refer in [12] to accuracy of those representations at closing as well as on the date of the agreement. In that context it would be more precise to require that the representations are accurate at signing and would, if made again at closing, be accurate at closing.

4.20 But if the seller makes its representations on the date of the agreement and at closing—in other words, if you use the recommended form of representations lead-in, example [1]—this wouldn't be an issue.

Excluding Representations Made on the Date of the Agreement

4.21　The seller might want to exclude from the bringdown condition, as in [12a], reference to seller representations made on the date of the agreement.[76] If the seller's representations are accurate at closing, this formulation would preclude the buyer from refusing to close because one or more seller representations had been inaccurate on the date of the agreement.

4.22　The seller would argue that this formulation is fair—that the buyer wouldn't be justified in refusing to close in those circumstances. If the buyer accepts this formulation, then the termination provisions shouldn't include as grounds for termination inaccuracies in the seller representations on the date of the agreement that prevent the bringdown condition from being satisfied— the seller's representations on entry into the contract would no longer be a factor in the bringdown condition. (See 6.9.)

4.23　If whatever caused the representations to be inaccurate at signing isn't remedied, under [12a] the buyer could refuse to close and presumably could terminate. (See 6.9.) And if the transaction doesn't close, the buyer could seek damages for inaccuracies in the seller's representations on the date of the agreement, although it might be that under the contract indemnification isn't available unless the transaction closes. (See 5.2.) So the buyer wouldn't be giving up anything significant by agreeing to the [12a] formulation.

4.24 But it also appears that the seller wouldn't be gaining very much by using [12a], as it's unlikely that a buyer would refuse to close based on inaccuracies in the seller's representations at signing if the representations would be accurate at closing. Indeed, a court might well decline to allow the buyer not to close in this context, regardless of how the bringdown condition is worded. So it's unlikely that anything meaningful is at stake.

Materiality

4.25 Usually the seller succeeds in having the buyer's bringdown condition be subject to a materiality qualification.[77] Often that's accomplished by having the condition require that the representations be *accurate in all material respects*,[78] but *materially accurate* is a more concise way of expressing the same concept. (See [12b].) It would be prudent to use *materially* as a defined term. (See 2.86.)

4.26 If, as is often the case, the bringdown condition to the buyer's obligations and the bringdown condition to the seller's obligations both incorporate a materiality qualification, *Materially* would need to be defined so as to apply to all parties. (See 2.88.) That in turn would require that each bringdown condition make it clear, as in [12c], from whose perspective materiality is determined.

4.27 If a bringdown condition incorporates a materiality qualification, it would be to the buyer's benefit to have it include the phrase

individually and in the aggregate, so that
materiality is determined by considering not
only the extent to which each representation
is inaccurate but also the cumulative effect
of all inaccuracies. Arguably that could be
accomplished by saying just *in the aggregate,*
but using the longer phrase makes it clearer
what is intended.

4.28   If you omit *individually and in the aggregate,*
the bringdown condition should refer to
each representation made by the Seller, as in
[12d]—that would serve to make it clear
that the cumulative effect of all inaccuracies
has no bearing on materiality.

4.29   A materiality qualification incorporated in
a bringdown condition is often phrased
using MAC, as in [12e].[79] But it's illogical
to think in terms of a representation
inaccuracy resulting in a MAC, given that
the only consequence of an inaccurate seller
representation would be that the buyer
is entitled not to close or has a claim for
indemnification. It's the facts underlying a
representation inaccuracy, rather than the
inaccuracy itself, that could result in a MAC.

4.30   The materiality qualification in a
bringdown condition can be subject to
carve-outs if the buyer is reluctant to have
the materiality qualification apply across
the board. A representation that is often
included in such carve-outs is the seller's
representation regarding its capitalization.[80]
This sort of carve-out would only make
sense if the representation itself did not
include a materiality qualification. More
generally, it's not clear that such carve-
outs accomplish much, as the notion of

the buyer's refusing to close because of an immaterial inaccuracy seems unpromising, whatever the representation.

4.31 Another issue related to materiality is "double materiality." It ostensibly arises when a materiality qualification is included in the bringdown condition to one party's obligation to close as well as in one or more representations of the other party.[81] The concern is apparently as follows: If the bringdown condition to the buyer's obligation to close incorporates a materiality qualification, then to determine whether that condition has been satisfied you apply a discount to the accuracy required for any given seller representation to be accurate. If a seller representation itself includes a materiality qualification, the same discount is also applied to the representation, with the result that the level of accuracy required to satisfy the bringdown condition is further reduced. Consequently, the buyer could be required to close even if a seller representation was on the date of the agreement, or is at closing, materially inaccurate.

4.32 It's common practice for drafters to seek to neutralize double materiality.[82] To do so, either they incorporate in the bringdown condition a materiality qualification only with respect to those representations that do not themselves contain a materiality qualification, as in [12f], or for purposes of the bringdown condition they strip out materiality qualifications from those representations that have them and apply instead a materiality qualification across the board, as in [12g].

4.33   But such contortions are unnecessary. If *material* conveys the "affects a decision" meaning (see 2.77)—and using the proposed definition of *Material* and *Materially* would make it clear that that's the case (see 2.86)—then materiality qualifications are not in fact equivalent to an across-the-board discount on accuracy, and materiality on materiality isn't equivalent to a discount on a discount. Instead, for purposes of determining both accuracy of a representation subject to a materiality qualification and satisfaction of a bringdown condition subject to a materiality qualification, one would consider the same external standard—whether the representation inaccuracy in question would have affected the buyer's decision to enter into the contract or would affect the buyer's decision to consummate the transaction. Because the same standard applies in both contexts, for purposes of determining satisfaction of the bringdown condition it's irrelevant whether the representation too contains a materiality qualification.

4.34   So the notion of double materiality is based on a misunderstanding of how materiality operates in M&A contracts. It should come as no surprise that caselaw makes no mention of double materiality—it's a figment of practitioner imagination.

4.35   Because courts don't recognize double materiality, attempting to neutralize it would seem to put a party in no worse a position than would have been the case had the issue been ignored. But the verbiage needed to address double materiality adds useless clutter. And to the extent that parties spend time negotiating double-materiality language, that's time wasted. Furthermore, assuming that double materiality is a valid concept requires a skewed view of materiality.

4.36 On the other hand, because courts don't recognize double materiality, not addressing it in contracts poses no risk. But you might find yourself wasting time in discussions with the other side over whether double materiality is a legitimate issue. Including the following provision in the boilerplate might save you some of that time by removing double materiality as a negotiation issue:

> **Double Materiality.** The parties acknowledge that regardless of whether any court recognizes it for purposes of other contracts, the contract-interpretation concept referred to as "double materiality" does not apply to this agreement, so the level of representation inaccuracy permitted by the materiality qualification to which section __ [the bringdown condition] is subject will not be affected by a materiality qualification to which any representation is subject.

4.37 So whether you address double materiality in a contract or seek to disregard it, you won't be assuming any risk but you may find that discussing the issue eats up some valuable time. Because addressing double materiality also serves to add clutter and perpetuates a confused view of materiality, disregarding double materiality would seem the more efficient option.

Stripping Out "Knowledge"

4.38   In some M&A contracts, it is specified in the bringdown condition that accuracy of the seller's representations is to be determined without giving effect to not only materiality but also knowledge qualifications. (Regarding knowledge qualifications, see 2.113.) In other words, the seller would get the benefit of a knowledge qualification for purposes of avoiding an indemnification claim but not for purposes of determining whether the buyer is required to close.

4.39   But such provisions are relatively rare: the author has determined that of the 106 contracts in the 2009 Private Target Deal Points Study sample (see "Preface—Features of this Book"), 90 contain a bringdown condition, and of those only two state that accuracy of the seller's representations is to be determined without giving effect to knowledge qualifications.

Reference-Point Exception

4.40   Bringdown conditions can contain other superfluous matter. For example, the exception in [12h] applies to representations that speak as of a specified date. This misconstrues the role of a reference point: including a reference point in a representation doesn't alter the fact that accuracy of that representation, along with all other representations, is determined on the date of the agreement and at closing (assuming that the representations lead-in resembles [1]). (See 2.58.)

THE COMPLIANCE-WITH-OBLIGATIONS CONDITION

4.41 As its name suggests, the compliance-with-obligations condition (see [13]) isn't satisfied unless the seller has complied with all preclosing obligations. (A given obligation could consist of a duty to do something or a duty *not* to do something. Instead of referring to *performance of* an obligation, this book refers to *compliance with* an obligation, as more clearly encompassing both action and inaction.)[83]

TABLE 8: THE COMPLIANCE-WITH-OBLIGATIONS CONDITION

[13]   ✓   that the Seller has complied with those of its obligations under this agreement that it is required to comply with before the Closing;

[13a]   that the Seller has Materially complied, individually and in the aggregate, with those of its obligations under this agreement that it is required to comply with before the Closing;

[13b]   that from the Buyer's perspective, the Seller has Materially complied, individually and in the aggregate, with those of its obligations under this agreement that it is required to comply with before the Closing;

[13c]   that the Seller has Materially complied
                  with each of its obligations under
                  this agreement that it is required to
                  comply with before the Closing;

4.42   Often the party required to satisfy the
            compliance-with-obligations condition
            will insist that the condition be subject to
            a materiality qualification. To incorporate
            materiality, it would be best to follow the
            principles discussed above with respect
            to the bringdown condition (see 4.25–
            28)—use *materially* as a defined term and
            decide whether to incorporate the phrase
            individually and in the aggregate (see [13a])
            or not (see [13c]). If the compliance-
            with-obligations condition to the buyer's
            obligation to close and the compliance-
            with-obligations condition to the seller's
            obligation to close both incorporate a
            materiality qualification or if for some other
            reason *Materially* is defined so as to apply to
            all parties (see 2.88), each compliance-with-
            obligations condition would need to make
            it clear, as in [13b], from whose perspective
            materiality is determined.

■ CHAPTER 5

Indemnification Provisions

5.1   Drafting a set of indemnification provisions involves addressing a range of issues. This book considers only those that involve interplay of categories of contract provisions.

WHAT LOSSES ARE INDEMNIFIED AGAINST

5.2   One such issue is what indemnifiable losses the seller would be indemnifying the buyer against. At a minimum, the buyer should require the seller to indemnify the buyer indemnified parties against any losses arising out of inaccuracy in any representations made by the seller and breach by the seller of any of its obligations. (But often indemnification provisions are drafted such that if the transaction fails to close, the buyer wouldn't be entitled to indemnification for inaccuracies in representations made at signing or breach of any obligations and instead would have to seek whatever other remedies are available.)[84]

5.3   Indemnification obligations shouldn't be subject to a materiality qualification: you can make representations subject to a materiality qualification (see 2.75) and make indemnification obligations subject to a basket (see 5.23), so there's no need to add yet another materiality escape hatch. And adding another layer of materiality would likely prompt further misguided hand-wringing over "double materiality." (See 4.31.)

5.4   If in its representations the seller discloses any event or circumstance that could result in postclosing liability, such as environmental contamination or pending litigation, the buyer may also want to require the seller to indemnify it against that liability, as otherwise the buyer wouldn't be covered.

PRECLOSING KNOWLEDGE OF INACCURATE REPRESENTATIONS

5.5   Before closing, the buyer might learn that one or more of the representations made by the seller at signing were inaccurate. For example, the seller might disclose any such inaccuracy to the buyer, perhaps in compliance with an obligation to inform the buyer of any event or circumstance that might preclude satisfaction of conditions to the buyer's obligation to close. (See 3.19.) And it might supply that information shortly before the anticipated closing, in the form of a "last-minute dump." Alternatively, the buyer might learn of the inaccuracy in the course of its due diligence. In the latter situation, the buyer might elect to close without informing the seller of its knowledge, with the idea of bringing a claim for indemnification—in other words, with the idea of "sandbagging" the seller.

5.6   Regardless of how the buyer came by its knowledge, the question is whether it is entitled to be indemnified for losses caused by the inaccurate representation. The caselaw on this issue is mixed,[85] so the cautious drafter should consider addressing explicitly the consequences of the buyer's knowing that a seller representation was inaccurate.

No-Indemnification-If-You-Know Provisions

5.7   Under the following provision, the buyer would not be entitled to be indemnified for an inaccurate seller representation if the buyer knew of that inaccuracy before the closing:

> **Knowledge of Inaccurate Representations.** The Seller is not required under section __ [Indemnification of the Buyer] to indemnify any Buyer Indemnified Party after the Closing for any Indemnifiable Loss arising out of an inaccurate representation made by the Seller in article __ if the Seller establishes that the Buyer had Knowledge of that inaccuracy before the Closing.

5.8   Such provisions are commonly referred to as "anti-sandbagging" provisions, although they wouldn't apply only to sandbagging—you could just as well call them "pro-last-minute-dump" provisions. A less loaded term would be "no-indemnification-if-you-know" provisions.

5.9   A more buyer-friendly version would refer to any knowledge the buyer had before signing, not just closing. A more seller-friendly version would include not only actual knowledge but constructive knowledge—knowledge that the buyer could have obtained by reasonably diligent investigation.[86]

5.10   Buyers strongly resist no-indemnification-if-you-know provisions.[87] For one thing, if the seller discloses inaccuracies after signing and the contract contains a no-indemnification-if-you-know provision, the buyer could be forced to choose between (1) not closing and bringing a claim for indemnification and (2) closing and forgoing indemnification. If the buyer has invested considerable resources in the transaction, that may have the effect of precluding it from walking away. And the buyer would likely feel that it should have the benefit of the bargain it made at signing, regardless of what it learns thereafter.

5.11   Also, such provisions have the effect of adding an element—the buyer's preclosing knowledge—to any claim seeking indemnification for inaccuracy in a seller representation.[88] In that regard, the above no-indemnification-if-you-know provision at least makes it clear that the burden is on the seller to prove that the buyer had that knowledge.

Indemnification-Even-If-You-Know Provisions

5.12   The opposite approach is reflected in what this book refers to as "indemnification-even-if-you-know" provisions, which state that the buyer is entitled to be indemnified for an inaccurate seller representation regardless of whether the buyer knew of that inaccuracy before the closing. Here is the form of indemnification-even-if-you-know provision that this book recommends:

Knowledge of Inaccurate Representations. The Seller's obligation under section __ [Indemnification of the Buyer] to indemnify any Buyer Indemnif-ied Party for any Indemnifiable Loss resulting from an inaccurate representation made by the Seller in article __ will not be affected if the Buyer has, or by reasonably diligent investigation could have obtained, Knowledge of that inaccuracy before the Closing.

5.13   For the buyer, the principal benefit of this provision is that it makes it less likely that the seller would raise the buyer's preclosing knowledge of representation inaccuracies as a defense against a claim for indemnification. It also makes it more likely that the buyer would prevail if the seller does raise such a defense. But the buyer shouldn't assume that an indemnification-even-if-you-know provision guarantees that it would be entitled to indemnification for losses caused by an inaccurate seller representation that the buyer knew about at signing, as opposed to at closing.[89] A cautious buyer would, before the contract is signed, try to use any such inaccuracy to get the seller to reduce the purchase price or grant the buyer a specific indemnity. (The buyer might want to use that approach even if the buyer learns of the inaccuracy after signing.)

5.14   Many contracts are silent as to the effect of preclosing knowledge of inaccurate representations. Presumably that's because "the picture of a Buyer lying in wait to hit an unsuspecting Seller with an indemnification claim as soon as the transaction closes is not a particularly attractive one"[90]—the buyer is unwilling to accept a no-indemnification-if-you-know provision but doesn't want to antagonize the seller by asking for an indemnification-even-if-you-know provision.

5.15   It would be difficult for the seller to come up with an economic argument against indemnification-even-if-you-know provisions.[91] But it would be to the seller's advantage if the buyer were to inform the seller before closing of any inaccuracy in the seller's representations that the seller hadn't been aware of—that would give the seller the opportunity to take steps aimed at ensuring that any representations that were inaccurate at signing are accurate when made again at closing. The cost of such remedial work might well be less than any claim for indemnification arising from the inaccurate representations.

5.16   So for the seller in fear of being sandbagged, an indemnification-even-if-you-know provision could be softened by requiring the buyer to disclose any inaccuracies in the seller's representations that the buyer is aware of at signing or becomes aware of after signing and before closing. That could be accomplished by means of (1) a representation with the date of the agreement as the reference point and (2) a preclosing obligation. Here are recommended forms of these provisions:

Buyer Representation

Inaccurate Seller Representations. On the date of this agreement, to the Buyer's Knowledge none of the representations made by the Seller in article __ is inaccurate [, except for any inaccuracies that would not reasonably be expected to result in a Material Adverse Change].

Buyer Preclosing Obligation

Inaccurate Seller Representations. The Buyer shall promptly notify the Seller if at any time before the Closing the Buyer acquires Knowledge, from any source other than the Seller or any of its representatives, of any inaccuracy in any of the representations made by the Seller in article __ [, except for any inaccuracies that would not reasonably be expected to result in a Material Adverse Change].

5.17 Note that this preclosing obligation imposed on the buyer is less exacting than the proposed form of obligation imposed on the seller to notify the buyer of any event or circumstance that would preclude, or would reasonably be expected to preclude, satisfaction of one or more conditions to the buyer's obligation to close. (See 3.19 and figure 4.) The obligation imposed on the buyer concerns only actual inaccuracies that the buyer learns of, not matters that might prevent the seller from making accurately at closing one or more representations. Given that the seller is in a better position to know about matters addressed in its representations, that difference in standards makes sense.

5.18 Of course, if the seller finds that it cannot ensure that any such inaccurate representation is accurate at closing, an indemnification-even-if-you-know provision would allow the buyer to bring a claim after closing—assuming that it elects to close—for any losses caused by that inaccuracy. The seller should be willing to live with that, given that it would have been spared the element of surprise. And from the buyer's perspective, the benefits of allowing the seller to take steps to ensure that a representation that was inaccurate on the date of the agreement is accurate at closing could well outstrip the uncertain value of the buyer's knowing that it could spring a claim for indemnification on the seller after closing.

MATERIALITY-SCRAPE PROVISIONS

5.19 Another indemnification provision with structural implications is the "materiality scrape" provision.[92] This pro-buyer provision states that when determining whether any representation is inaccurate for purposes of the seller's indemnification obligations, or determining the amount of damages arising from that inaccuracy, or both, any materiality qualification is to be disregarded.

5.20 For example, if (1) the seller represents that its premises have no environmental contamination, except for any contamination that would not reasonably be expected to result in a MAC, and (2) the contract contains a materiality scrape-provision, for indemnification purposes the MAC qualification would be ignored.

5.21   But materiality-scrape provisions present two shortcomings. First, scraping the materiality from some provisions is problematic. It's impossible to strip MAC from a representation regarding nonoccurrence of a MAC since a given date—for example, *Since December 31, 2009, no MAC has occurred.* And if in a given representation *material* can't be replaced with MAC (see 2.97), a materiality-scrape provision might well change the meaning of the representation in a way that goes beyond indicating that for purposes of the bringdown condition the buyer isn't inclined to cut the seller any slack. For example, stripping materiality from the representation *Schedule 4.2 contains a list of the Seller's material contracts* would presumably render it inaccurate when made.

5.22   But materiality-scrape provisions suffer from a more fundamental shortcoming. In any M&A contract that contains a bringdown condition subject to a materiality qualification—and that's the vast majority of them (see 4.25)—any materiality exceptions in the representations serve only to limit the representing party's indemnification obligations. (If the bringdown condition is subject to a materiality qualification, materiality exceptions in the representations wouldn't be necessary to prevent the other party from walking from the deal because of an immaterial inaccuracy in a representation.)

So including a materiality-scrape provision would serve to eliminate the sole function served by materiality exceptions.

5.23   It follows that it would be much more efficient instead to (1) eliminate both the materiality-scrape provision and some or all representation qualifications relating to significance and (2) make any seller indemnification obligations subject to a basket. (A basket is a threshold, expressed as a dollar amount, that indemnifiable losses must reach before the seller's indemnification obligation is triggered.)[93] The basket would be the buyer's principal, or sole, protection against being subject to indemnification claims for relatively minor inaccuracies in its representations. (See 2.111.)

FILLING THE BASKET WITH SIGNIFICANCE-QUALIFICATION LOSSES

5.24   In theory, one variation on materiality-scrape provisions could be of use even in a contract that contains a bringdown condition incorporating a materiality qualification.

5.25   In negotiations, a buyer might accept that the seller's indemnification obligations will be subject to a basket, and then find itself allowing the seller to add significance qualifications (using *Material*, MAC, or *Significant*) to various representations. (See 2.75.) The buyer could seek to offset those concessions by asking the seller to add the following to the indemnification provisions relating to the basket:

If an Indemnified Party incurs losses that, but for a materiality or other significance qualification in one or more representations, would constitute Indemnifiable Losses, those losses will be deemed Indemnifiable Losses for purposes of determining whether the dollar limit specified in this section __ [Basket] has been reached.

5.26   This provision would ensure that if any significance qualification results in the buyer's incurring losses for which it isn't indemnified, those losses would serve to "fill" the basket more quickly, but the buyer couldn't use them as the basis for a claim for indemnification. (See figure 3.) The seller would likely prefer this provision to simply reducing the amount of the basket—the haircut represented by using losses to fill the basket would apply to only a limited range of indemnification claims, whereas reducing the amount of the basket would apply to all indemnification claims.

5.27   But that said, reducing the basket would be simpler. And simpler still would be omitting some or all qualifications relating to significance and adjusting the basket accordingly. (See 5.23.)

■ CHAPTER 6

Termination Provisions

6.1   Although commentators have paid less attention to termination provisions than to the other categories of provisions,[94] being able to terminate a transaction before the closing is as essential to the logic of an M&A contract as being able to consummate the transaction. And as is the case with other categories of provisions, termination provisions cannot be considered in isolation.

STAND-ALONE AND CONDITION-LINKED TERMINATION PROVISIONS

6.2   To better understand the function of termination provisions, it helps to divide them into two subcategories. The first subcategory, "stand-alone" termination provisions, is unrelated to other categories of contract provisions. Viewed from the buyer's perspective, stand-alone termination provisions include the right to terminate (1) on agreement of the parties; (2) on the "drop-dead date"; (3) if the buyer isn't satisfied with the results of its due diligence; and (4) if the seller elects to proceed with an alternative transaction. (See figure 6.) The first two are standard, whatever the transaction; the latter two are transaction-specific.

FIGURE 6: TERMINATION PROVISIONS

This table contains provisions stating when the buyer would be permitted to terminate. Some of the provisions also apply to the seller, but provisions that apply only to the seller have been omitted.

Most provisions would be appropriate in all contracts; those that are transaction-specific are designated "EXAMPLE."

Lead-in: This agreement may be terminated as follows:		
Stand-Alone Termination Provisions		*Comments*
by written agreement of the parties;		Even without this provision, the parties could elect to terminate.
by the Buyer or the Seller if the Closing has not occurred by the Termination Date, except that the right to terminate this agreement in accordance with this clause (2) will not be available to any party whose failure to comply with any obligation under this agreement resulted in the Closing not occurring by the Termination Date;		The termination date is often referred to as the "drop-dead date."
EXAMPLE: by the Buyer if for any reason it is not satisfied with the results of its due diligence investigation of the Seller;		
EXAMPLE: by the Buyer if the Seller's board of directors authorizes the Seller to enter into an Alternative Transaction or withdraws the Seller Board Recommendation;		
Related Conditions	*Termination Provisions that Refer to Inability to Satisfy a Condition*	*Comments*
Bringdown condition	by the Buyer, if any representation made by the Seller in article __ on the date of this agreement was inaccurate when made such that the condition stated in section __ [the "bringdown" condition] could not be satisfied;	These are an alternative to a more conventional formulation—"by the Buyer, if any representation of the Seller stated in this agreement was inaccurate when made or becomes inaccurate such that the condition stated in section __ [the bringdown condition] would not be satisfied."
Bringdown condition	by the Buyer, if any representation made by the Seller in article 2 as of the date of this agreement could not be made again on any date after the date of this agreement and before the Termination Date so as to satisfy the condition stated in section __ [the bringdown condition] (assuming for that purpose that that date is the Closing Date), except that if the Seller is capable of remedying the circumstances preventing that condition from being satisfied, then the Buyer may not terminate this agreement in accordance with this clause x unless the Buyer notifies the Seller of those circumstances and the Seller fails to remedy those circumstances no later than 10 days after the Buyer so notifies the Seller;	
Compliance-with-obligations condition	by the Buyer, if the Seller fails to comply with any of its obligations under this agreement such that the condition stated in section __ [the compliance-with-obligations condition] could not be satisfied;	

100

FIGURE 6: TERMINATION PROVISIONS
(continued)

Related Condition	Termination Provisions that Track the Language of a Condition	Comments
Gap-closing condition relating to absence of a MAC since the date of the agreement	EXAMPLE: by the Buyer, if a MAC has occurred since the date of this agreement;	
Related Conditions	**Termination Provisions Specifying an Event that Would Prevent a Given Condition from Being Satisfied**	**Comments**
Gating condition regarding shareholder authorization	EXAMPLE: by the Buyer or the Seller if at the Special Meeting or any adjournment thereof the Seller Shareholder Approval is not obtained;	This is an example of a termination provision that refers an event that would prevent a gating condition from being satisfied.
External conditions that no law or order in effect	by the Buyer or the Seller if any Order permanently enjoining or otherwise prohibiting consummation of the transaction contemplated by this agreement becomes final and nonappealable, on condition that a party wishing to terminate this agreement in accordance with this clause (2) has complied with section ___ [the ensure-the-conditions-are-satisfied obligation] with respect to satisfaction of the condition stated in section ___ [the condition stating that that there is in effect no Law or Order that prevents consummation of the Transaction];	This also in effect serves as a stand-alone termination provision that addresses the issue raised by the condition as to the absence of any proceedings that seek to prevent consummation of the transaction; see figure 7.
	Redundant Termination Provisions	
	EXAMPLE: by the Buyer if there occurs an Event of Bankruptcy with respect to the Seller;	This would presumably be covered by a "Solvency" representation given by the seller. (Note that a court may well hold that termination in the event of bankruptcy is unenforceable.)

6.3 The second subcategory of termination provisions is those that are linked to conditions, either by referring to the inability to satisfy a condition, by tracking the language of a condition, or by specifying an event that would preclude a condition from being satisfied. (See figure 6.) If the buyer determines that a given condition cannot be satisfied, it would want to have the right to terminate then rather than have to wait until the drop-dead date. Terminating sooner would likely reduce the buyer's transaction costs and allow it to move on to other matters.

THE LINK BETWEEN CONDITIONS AND TERMINATION PROVISIONS

6.4 Seemingly the simplest way to give the buyer a right to terminate linked to conditions would be by means of a catch-all provision stating that the buyer may terminate the contract if it would not be possible to satisfy any one or more conditions to the buyer's obligation to close.[95] Alternatively, a given termination provision could state that the buyer may terminate if a specified condition could not be satisfied.

6.5 But there are shortcomings to stating that the buyer may terminate if a condition cannot be satisfied, and understanding those shortcomings requires considering two groups of conditions: First, conditions other than the bringdown condition and the compliance-with-obligations condition. And second, the bringdown condition and the compliance-with-obligations condition.

6.6 With respect to conditions falling within the first group, it's problematic to base a termination provision on inability to satisfy any such condition. Instead, it's preferable to track the language of the condition, specify an event that would preclude the condition from being satisfied, or simply forgo basing a termination provision on that condition, with the appropriate approach depending on the condition. (See figure 7.)

6.7 But a different analysis applies to the bringdown condition and the compliance-with-obligations condition. Those conditions are omnibus provisions that apply to all seller representations and preclosing obligations, respectively, so for purposes of a linked termination provision you have only two choices: either track the language of the condition or refer to inability to satisfy the condition in question.

6.8 If the bringdown condition and compliance-with-obligations condition incorporate a materiality qualification, as is usually the case, tracking the language of the condition would be unwieldy and could result in inconsistency between the condition and the termination provision.

6.9 Furthermore, the bringdown condition should give rise to two termination provisions—you would need to address separately, as shown in figure 6, representations made on the date of the agreement and representations to be made at closing. The provision regarding representations made on the date of the

FIGURE 7: THE LINK BETWEEN CONDITIONS AND TERMINATION PROVISIONS

A buyer would want the right to terminate if any closing condition couldn't be satisfied. But in the case of conditions other than the bringdown condition and the compliance-with-obligations condition, various factors make it preferable not to state, in a catch-all termination provision or in individual termination provisions, that the buyer may terminate if any one of those conditions cannot be satisfied. As explored in this table, the factors vary depending on the kind of condition. Shading indicates contract language; the unshaded text represents analysis.

Condition		Termination Provision
Condition that states that a specified event has to have taken place	EXAMPLE: that the Seller has obtained all [Material] Consents;	by the Buyer if the condition stated in section ___ could not be satisfied;
		by the Buyer if any Person from whom the Seller is seeking a [Material] Consent refuses in writing to give that [Material] Consent;

ANALYSIS: With respect to this kind of condition, nonoccurrence of the specified event wouldn't necessarily mean that the condition couldn't be satisfied—it could just mean that it hasn't been satisfied yet. So if the buyer wants to terminate by invoking a termination provision that allows the buyer to terminate if any condition, or a specific condition, couldn't be satisfied, the buyer would have to argue that some other event precludes satisfaction of this kind of condition. With respect to the example condition above, the buyer could point to a landlord's having stated in writing that it won't grant a consent.

But that approach raises the possibility of dispute. With respect to the example condition above, the seller could claim that it should have until the drop-dead date to get the landlord to change its mind. To avoid such uncertainty, instead of saying that failure to satisfy a given condition is grounds for termination, it would be clearer to specify in a termination provision—as in the example termination provision above—any one or more events that would have the effect of preventing that condition from being satisfied.

Condition that states that a specified event has to have NOT taken place	EXAMPLE: that no MAC has occurred since the date of this agreement;	by the Buyer if the condition stated in section ___ could not be satisfied;
		by the Buyer if a MAC has occurred since the date of the agreement;

ANALYSIS: Unlike conditions that specify that an event has to have taken place, this kind of condition would be impossible to satisfy once the specified event takes place, so the termination provision could simply cross-reference the condition. But for clarity and ease of reading, it would be preferable to do without the cross-reference and instead track the language of the condition.

Condition that states that a specified circumstance has to be in effect	EXAMPLE: that the market price of the Seller's common stock is at least $23.00;	by the Buyer if the condition stated in section ___ could not be satisfied;

ANALYSIS: If a condition specifies a circumstance that has to be in effect, absence of that circumstance preclosing wouldn't mean that the condition couldn't be satisfied—it would just mean that it couldn't be satisfied at that point. So if with respect to this sort of condition the buyer wants to terminate by invoking a termination provision that allows the buyer to terminate if any condition, or a specific condition, couldn't be satisfied, the buyer would have to argue that some other event precludes satisfaction of the condition. But with respect to the example condition above, it's not clear what kind of event that might be, and any such event would likely be sufficiently drastic as to be covered somewhere else in the contract. So it's likely that with respect to the example condition above, nothing would be gained by linking a termination provision to this condition. But this sort of analysis should be applied to such conditions on a case-by-case basis.

FIGURE 7: THE LINK BETWEEN CONDITIONS AND TERMINATION PROVISIONS (continued)

Condition		Termination Provision
Condition that states that a specified circumstance has to NOT be in effect	EXAMPLE: that there is in effect no Law or Order that prevents consummation of the Transaction;	by the Buyer if the condition stated in section ― could not be satisfied;
	EXAMPLE: that no Proceedings are pending that seek to prevent consummation of the Transaction;	by the Buyer or the Seller if any Order permanently enjoining or otherwise prohibiting consummation of the transaction contemplated by this agreement becomes final and nonappealable ... ;

ANALYSIS: If a condition specifies a circumstance that has to not be in effect, having that circumstance be in effect preclosing wouldn't mean that the condition couldn't be satisfied—it would just mean that it couldn't be satisfied at that point. So if with respect to this sort of condition the buyer wants to terminate by invoking a termination provision that allows the buyer to terminate if any condition, or a specific condition, couldn't be satisfied, the buyer would have to argue that some other event precludes satisfaction of the condition. It would be clearer instead to specify any such event in a termination provision. That's what the example termination provision above does for purposes of the first example condition above, with respect to court orders.

And the second example condition above shows that whether this sort of condition can be satisfied might have no bearing on the buyer's concerns with respect to the topic addressed in the condition: it may be that no proceedings are pending against the seller because proceedings that had been pending have concluded, with the seller having lost. So to address in a termination provision the buyer's concerns regarding the issue addressed in this condition would require a stand-alone termination provision. It so happens that the termination provision offered with respect the first example condition above would also address the issue raised with respect to the second example condition above. But how to treat this kind of condition should be considered on a case-by-case basis.

agreement is straightforward, because those representations will have already been made. (It should be omitted if the bringdown condition omits any mention of seller representations made on the date of the agreement. See 4.22.) By contrast, closing-date representations won't have been made yet, so the question is whether they could be made accurately at any given point after signing. And you also have to take into account the possibility of rectifying whatever is precluding having the representation be accurate when made at closing. That added complexity precludes simply tracking the language of the bringdown condition.

6.10 Instead of such a bifurcated arrangement, drafters often use formulations comparable to the following: "by the Buyer, if any representation of the Seller stated in this agreement was inaccurate when made or becomes inaccurate such that the condition stated in section __ [the bringdown condition] would not be satisfied." The problem with this approach is that a representation made on the date of the agreement is immutably accurate or inaccurate—it cannot thereafter become inaccurate due to changes occurring after the date of the agreement. (See 2.9.) You should instead treat separately the representations to be made at closing.

6.11 What if the seller fails to make reasonable efforts to rectify circumstances that would prevent satisfaction of the bringdown condition? If the contract contains an ensure-the-conditions-are-satisfied obligation (see 3.6), the buyer might—depending on how the compliance-with-obligations condition is worded—be able to terminate the agreement on the grounds that the seller has failed to comply with a preclosing obligation. That might permit the buyer to terminate sooner than if it were to terminate because the bringdown condition couldn't be satisfied.

REDUNDANCY

6.12   The principal source of redundancy in termination provisions is those provisions that relate to matters already addressed in representations. For example, if the seller represents that X has not occurred, it would be redundant to add a termination provision stating that the buyer may terminate if X occurs—it would be entitled to do so regardless, because occurrence of that event would mean that the bringdown condition could not be satisfied (assuming that any materiality threshold in the bringdown condition had been exceeded). Figure 6 provides an example of such a redundant termination provision.

Endnotes

Click on the number at the beginning of any endnote to go the corresponding endnote number in the text, and vice versa.

1   KENNETH A. ADAMS, A MANUAL OF STYLE FOR CONTRACT DRAFTING (2d ed. 2008).

2   *See* LOU R. KLING & EILEEN T. NUGENT, NEGOTIATED ACQUISITIONS OF COMPANIES, SUBSIDIARIES AND DIVISIONS § 1.02 (2011) [hereinafter KLING & NUGENT].

3   American Bar Association Mergers & Acquisitions Market Trends Subcommittee, 2009 Private Target Mergers & Acquisitions Deal Points Study (Dec. 23, 2009) [hereinafter 2009 Private Target Deal Points Study] (available only to members of the Committee on Mergers and Acquisitions at http://link.reuters.com/muc78q).

4   Accessible only to members of the Committee on Mergers and Acquisitions at http://link.reuters.com/ked78q.

5   Kenneth A. Adams, *Dysfunctional Drafting*, Nat'l L.J., Sept. 8, 2008.

6   *See* KLING & NUGENT, *supra* note 2, § 1.05[1].

7   *See* BLACK'S LAW DICTIONARY (9th ed. 2009), *available at* Westlaw for "representation".

8   *See* KLING & NUGENT, *supra* note 2, § 15.02.

9   *See id.* § 15.01 n.1.

10   *See* JAMES C. FREUND, ANATOMY OF A MERGER: STRATEGIES AND TECHNIQUES FOR NEGOTIATING CORPORATE ACQUISITIONS, § 5.3.1 (1975).

11   *See* KLING & NUGENT, *supra* note 2, § 15.02[4]; NEGOTIATING AND DRAFTING CONTRACT BOILERPLATE 288 (Tina L. Stark ed. 2003).

12   *See id.* § 14.02[6].

13   *See id.* § 11.01[3] (suggesting, with respect to the representation *The Company, as of the date of this Agreement, is and, as of the Closing Date, will be in compliance with all laws applicable to it,* that if as of the Closing Date the Company is not in compliance with all laws, the buyer could "claim a breach and sue for damages").

14   *See id.* § 14.02[5] ("[T]he certificate is needed in addition to the bringdown. How else will the Buyer know that the representations are true at closing and the bringdown condition is satisfied?").

15   *See, e.g.,* STANLEY FOSTER REED, ALEXANDER REED LAJOUX, H. PETER NESVOLD, THE ART OF M&A: A MERGER ACQUISITION BUYOUT GUIDE 481 (4th ed. 2007) (stating that the officer's certificate "has another very important effect: it is a restatement of all the representations and warranties as of the closing date" and that "[i]f the certificate is not accurate, the inaccuracy will constitute a breach of a representation or warranty and may give rise to liability from buyer to seller under the Indemnity section of the agreement").

16   *See* FREUND, *supra* note 10, § 5.3.2 (noting that if a representation is made only as of the date of the agreement and circumstances have changed by the time the closing occurs, then "although the purchaser might well have a rescission remedy and other rights under Rule 10b-5 (as well as personal claims against the fraudulent officer and the negligent attorney), the purchaser's right to indemnification under the agreement is questionable— since the representation was true when made, and the lawyer's opinion, the officer's certificate, and the reiteration of representations are all merely closing conditions serving a different purpose in the overall scheme of things").

17   *See* I COMMITTEE ON MERGERS AND ACQUISITIONS, SECTION OF BUSINESS LAW, AMERICAN BAR ASSOCIATION, MODEL STOCK PURCHASE AGREEMENT 253 (2011) [hereinafter MODEL STOCK PURCHASE AGREEMENT].

18   *See* KLING & NUGENT, *supra* note 2, § 14.02 n.22

("However, if a false certificate is delivered, stating that all the representations and warranties are true at closing when in fact they are not, then the indemnification provisions (if any) or a fraud claim (if the requisites are satisfied) will generally provide the nonrepresenting party with redress.").

19 *See* MODEL STOCK PURCHASE AGREEMENT, *supra* note 17, at 312.

20 *See* ABRY Partners V, L.P. v. F & W Acquisition LLC, <u>891 A.2d 1032</u>, 1051 (Del. Ch. 2006)(assuming, for purposes of a motion for summary judgment in an action not for indemnification but for rescission of a stock purchase agreement, that "the complaint sets forth facts supporting an inference that the Company made misrepresentations in its financial statements, the accuracy of which was represented and warranted in the Stock Purchase Agreement by the Company and *in the Officer's Certificate by the Seller*" (emphasis added)).

21 *See* ADAMS, *supra* note 1, ¶ 12.65–68 (discussing use of *deem*).

22 *See* Kenneth A. Adams, <u>*Revisiting the Meaning of "Closing,"*</u> AdamsDrafting Blog (Feb. 22, 2011).

23 *See, e.g.*, TINA L. STARK, DRAFTING CONTRACTS: HOW LAWYERS DO WHAT THEY DO 13 (2007) ("By virtue of [the line "The Seller *represents and warrants* to the Buyer as follows"], every statement in the sections that followed would be both a representation and a warranty.").

24 *See* Kenneth A. Adams, <u>*Defining "Magic Words" and Related Terminology*</u>, AdamsDrafting Blog (Apr. 13, 2011).

25 *See* Adams, *supra* note 1, ¶ 16.11.

26 *See id.* ¶ 12.299; Glenn D. West & Kim M. Shah, *Debunking the Myth of the Sandbagging Buyer: When Sellers Ask Buyers to Agree to Anti-Sandbagging Clauses, Who Is Sandbagging Whom?*, M&A Law., Jan. 2007, at 3, *available at* <u>Westlaw 11 No. 1 GLMALAW 3</u> (noting that "there is no longer any distinction in contract between a warranty, a representation, and a separately indemnifiable matter

in the U.S. (if there ever was)"); Kenneth A. Adams, *"Representations and Warranties"—Glenn West Wades In*, AdamsDrafting Blog (Sept. 25, 2009).

27   *See* Kenneth A. Adams, *Glenn West Reopens the "Represents and Warrants" Can of Worms!*, AdamsDrafting Blog (Dec. 30, 2009).

28   *See* ADAMS, *supra* note 1, ¶ 12.302.

29   *See id.* ¶ 12.226.

30   *See id.* ¶ 2.11.

31   *See id.* ¶ 2.188.

32   *See id.* ¶ 16.7–10 (on using verbs instead of abstract nouns).

33   *See* John F. Seegal, *Allocation of Post-Closing Risk in Private Company Acquisitions*, in ACQUIRING OR SELLNG THE PRIVATELY HELD COMPANY 2009 639, 667 (PLI Corp. L. and Prac. Course Handbook Series No. 1742), *available at* Westlaw 1742 PLI/Corp 639 (including as exhibit K a "Seller-oriented facing page for the disclosure schedule").

34   *See, e.g.*, MODEL STOCK PURCHASE AGREEMENT, *supra* note 17, at 82 (using as the lead-in to the sellers' representations "Sellers, jointly and severally, represent and warrant to Buyer as follows").

35   *See* BLACK'S LAW DICTIONARY, *supra* note 7, *available at* Westlaw for "joint and several liability".

36   *See* ADAMS, *supra* note 1, ¶¶ 12.159–161.

37   *See id.* ¶¶ 9.14–18.

38   *See* KLING & NUGENT, *supra* note 2, § 11.01[3].

39   *See* ADAMS, *supra* note 1, ¶ 2.112.

40   KLING & NUGENT, *supra* note 2, § 10.01.

41   *See id.* § 10.02 n.2.

42   This section is derived from chapter 8 of ADAMS, *supra* note 1.

43   *See* ADAMS, *supra* note 1, ¶¶ 6.3–7, ¶¶ 6.15–18 (distinguishing vagueness and ambiguity).

44   <u>789 A.2d 14</u>, 68 (Del. Ch. 2001).

45   *See* Hexion Specialty Chems., Inc. v. Huntsman Corp., <u>965 A.2d 715</u> (Del. Ch. 2008) ("A buyer faces a heavy burden when it attempts to invoke a material adverse effect clause in order to avoid its obligation to close.")

46   Definition of the Term Significant Deficiency, Securities Act Release No. 8829, Exchange Act Release No. 56203, <u>17 C.F.R. pt. 210</u>, 240 (2007).

47   *See* ADAMS, *supra* note 1, ¶ 8.57, ¶ 8.64.

48   *See id.* ¶¶ 8.60–63.

49   For further guidance on this subject, see ADAMS, *supra* note 1, ¶¶ 8.67–128.

50   *See* 2009 Private Target Deal Points Study, *supra* note 3, at 28 (noting that only 38% of the sample contracts that contain a definition of *material adverse effect* include *prospects* in the definition).

51   *See* <u>KLING & NUGENT</u>, *supra* note 2, § 11.03[2].

52   *See* <u>id.</u>

53   *See* <u>id.</u> § 11.02.

54   *See* ADAMS, *supra* note 1, ¶ 12.162.

55   *See id.* ¶¶ 5.13–32 (describing autonomous definitions).

56   *See* <u>KLING & NUGENT</u>, *supra* note 2, § 11.02.

57   *See* <u>id.</u>

58   *See* ADAMS, *supra* note 1, ¶¶ 12.316.

59   *See id.* ¶¶ 7.5–17.

60   *See id.* ¶¶ 7.18–27.

61   *See id.* ¶¶ 7.29–30.

62   *See id.* ¶ 7.31.

63   *See* Kenneth A. Adams, *"Best Efforts" Under Canadian Law: Once More, With Feeling,* AdamsDrafting Blog (June 10, 2011).

64   *See* ADAMS, *supra* note 1, ¶¶ 7.45–55.

65   *See id.* ¶¶ 7.50–55.

66   *See* KLING & NUGENT, *supra* note 2, § 13.01.

67   *See id.* § 13.02[4].

68   The discussion in 3.20–24 is derived from Kenneth A. Adams, *How to Avoid Contractual Train Wrecks,* Nat'l. L.J., Nov. 6, 2006, at S1, *available at* Westlaw 11/6/2006 NLJ S1, (Col. 1), (Col. 1).

69   *See* 13 RICHARD A. LORD, WILLISTON ON CONTRACTS § 39:17.

70   *See* KLING & NUGENT, *supra* note 2, § 14.01 n.5.

71   *See id.* § 14.01.

72   *See* BLACK'S LAW DICTIONARY, *supra* note 7, *available at* Westlaw for "condition subsequent".

73   *See* Restatement (Second) of Contracts § 224 cmt. e and reporter's notes (1981); *see id.* § 230 reporter's notes.

74   *See* ADAMS, *supra* note 1, ¶ 2.178.

75   *See* KENNETH A. ADAMS, *Revisiting the Meaning of "Closing,"* AdamsDrafting Blog (Feb. 22, 2011), (proposing new language for such a provision).

76   *See* KLING & NUGENT, *supra* note 2, § 14.02[1]; *see also* 2009 Private Target Deal Points Study, *supra* note 3,

at 58 (noting that of those contracts in the study sample that contain a bringdown condition, 34% omit any from the bringdown condition reference to accuracy of representations at signing).

77   *See id.* at 60 (noting that of the contracts in the study sample that contained a bringdown condition that referred to accuracy at closing, only 8% did not include a materiality qualification).

78   *See id.*

79   *See id.*

80   *See id.* at 61–62.

81   *See* KLING & NUGENT, *supra* note 2, § 11.03[3], KLING & NUGENT § 14.02[3]; Seegal, *supra* note 33, at 615.

82   *See* 2009 Private Target Deal Points Study, *supra* note 3, at 64 (noting that of the contracts in the study sample that contain a bringdown condition, most seek to address double materiality in the bringdown condition).

83   *See* ADAMS, *supra* note 1, ¶ 12.235.

84   *See* KLING & NUGENT, *supra* note 2, § 15.01.

85   *See* ADAMS, *supra* note 68, at S1; Robert F. Quaintance, Jr., *Can You Sandbag? When a Buyer Knows Seller's Reps and Warranties Are Untrue,* M&A Law., Mar. 2003, at 8, *available at* Westlaw 5 No. 9 GLMALAW 8.

86   *See* 2009 Private Target Deal Points Study, *supra* note 3, at 77 (noting that of those contracts in the sample that provide for a deferred closing, 13% contain an "anti-sandbagging" provision that refers to actual and constructive knowledge).

87   *See id.* at 76 (noting that out of the contracts included in the study sample, 8% included an "anti-sandbagging" clause, 39% included a "pro-sandbagging" clause, and 53% were silent).

88   *See* KLING & NUGENT, *supra* note 2, § 15.02[2].

89   *See*, Quaintance *supra* note 85.

90   *See* Kling & Nugent, *supra* note 2, § 15.02[2].

91   *See id.* (noting with respect to sandbagging that "the economics of the situation are really no different than ... where the Seller was aware of the problem and supplemented its disclosure schedule").

92   *See* John LeClaire, Hovey Kemp, Mike Kendall & A.J. Weidhass, *Scraping By*, Mergers & Acquisitions, July 2008, *available at* Westlaw 7/1/08 DEALMAKERS; *see also* 2009 Private Target Deal Points Study, *supra* note 3, at 98 (noting that of those contracts in the study sample that provided for baskets, 24% contained materiality-scrape provisions).

93   *See* Kling & Nugent, *supra* note 2, § 15.03[1]; Negotiating and Drafting Contract Boilerplate, *supra* note 11, § 10.10.

94   *See, e.g.*, Freund, *supra* note 10, § 5.3.1 (referring to representations, preclosing obligations, conditions, and indemnification as the "four horsemen" but not mentioning termination provisions).

95   *See, e.g.*, Model Stock Purchase Agreement, *supra* note 17, at 276 (stating that Buyer may terminate the agreement "if satisfaction of any condition in Article 8 by _____ or such later date as the parties may agree upon ... becomes impossible").